YOUNG WRITERS

Spellbound

NORTH EAST ENGLAND

Poetry Now

YOUNG WRITERS

Edited by Jenny Edwards

First published in Great Britain in 1998 by
POETRY NOW YOUNG WRITERS
1-2 Wainman Road, Woodston,
Peterborough, PE2 7BU
Telephone (01733) 230748

HB ISBN 1 86188 812 0
SB ISBN 1 86188 817 1

FOREWORD

In this, our 5th competition year, we are proud to present *Spellbound North East England*. This anthology represents the very best endeavours of the children from this region.

The standard of entries was high, which made the task of editing a difficult one, but nonetheless enjoyable. The variety of subject matter, creativity and imagination never ceases to amaze and is indeed an inspiration to us all.

This year's competition attracted the highest entry ever - over 46,000 from all over the UK, and for the first time included entries from English speaking children living abroad.

Congratulations to all the writers published in *Spellbound North East England*. We hope you enjoy reading the poems and that your success will inspire you to continue writing in the future.

CONTENTS

Marden High School

Catriona Rutherford	20
Helen Lockey	21
Kate Hudson	22
Elin Wallis	22
Vicky Ellison	23
Nicola Gordon	24
Fiona O'Keefe	25
Keith Patterson	26
Emma Murray	27
Catriona Atkinson	28

St Anthony's Girls' School

Andrea Dietz	29
Nicola James	29
Clare Ricketts	30
Samantha Spraggon	31
Laura Conlon	31
Lindsey Bell	32
Helen Wilson	33
Laura Kelly	34
Katie Roddy	34
Laura Gulliver	35
Cristina Nethercott	35
Claire Maughan	36
Jennifer Bayley	36
Zoe Greenfield	37
Catherine Taroni	38
Mitra Akrami	39
Emma J Matthews	39
Helen Thompson	40
Rebecca Atkinson	41
Joanna Kerr	42

Neil Sewell	61
Billy McIver	62
David Henderson	63
Zoë Barwick	64
Jonathan Parr	64
Michelle McBeth	65
Daniel Butler	66
Liberty Woodward	67
Alia Saidan	67
Andrew Nesbitt	68
Andrew Turnbull	69
Andrew Hall	70
Leanne Thomasson	70
Katie Watson	71
Ian Batey	72
Nicholas Furno	72
Duncan Wild	73
Robert Slone	74
Adam Jobson	75
Steven Lee	75
Neil Leggett	76
Ross Fletcher	77
Elayne Chapman	77
Kate Robertson	78
Holly Hakin	79
Andrew Hodgson	79
Victoria Rodriguez	80
Nicholas Jackson	80
Christopher Hall	81
Robert Chivers	81
Katie Hedquist	82
Louise Adie	83
Shaun Kirkby	84
Leanne Proud	84
Heather Wade	85

James Sanders	85
Anthony Stobbs	86
Sarah Brown	86
Chris Stewart	87
Maria Mather	87
Sarah Madgwick	88
Amanda Elsdon	88
Joanne Harvey	89
Rachelle Whillis	90
Richard Anderson	90
Christine Rooney	91
Anna Smith	91
Steven Wray	92
Claire Allen	93
Ben Walker	93
Andrew Smith	94
Shaun Whillis	94
Amy Scullion	95
Louise Pocklington	96
Zoe Connors	96
Adele Corke	97
Chloé Gannon	98
Steven Wood	98
Linzi Anderson	99
Lee Lannen	100
Alexander McIsaac	101
Ashlie Morse	101
Emma O'Neill	102
Laura Tindle	102
Judith Brown	103
Jade Coleman	104
Mark Reay	104
Cheryl Robinson	105
Sarah Milne	106
Christina Jackson	106

Usworth Comprehensive School

Amy Hurst	202
Sharrie Muter	202
Kevin Bestford	203
Helen Syme	203
Malcolm Nevins	204
Amy Fletcher	204
Rachael Gibson	205
Danielle Fairweather	206
Joanne Bainbridge	207
Kayleigh Ingham	207
Joanne Quigley	208
Vicky Litster	208
Kathryn Sawyers	209
Gillian Stewart	210
Scott Brown	211
Victoria Kirtley	212
Nicholas Bell	212
Lucy Barber	213
Adam Dixon	214
Sara Lang	214
Suzanne Cook	215
Gary Routledge	216
Kayleigh Underwood	217

Western Middle School

Laura Bertram	218
Jessica Fairs	220
Katy Barron	221
Mel McCartney	222

Whitburn Comprehensive School

Deborah Philpot	223
Stacey Judd	223
Hannah Forster	224

THE POEMS

THE TWO SIDES TO THE SEA

Cold and dull, and always so violent,

> But bright and warm, quite motionless.

It's a killer, a vandal, even a destroyer,

> Then so soft and gentle, most leisurable.

The great waves, so merciless and powerful,

> Before the tame and peaceful ripples,
> humane and docile.

With each step you take into the mighty
ocean comes a chance more mortal than
the vastness of the sea itself.
You will be pursued by the living creatures,
belonging to that particular realm till you
depart.

> Or can it co-operate? It may well seldom
> but it can.

It will condemn for any mistake, so one will
receive the punishment required, whether it
be a petty or a tidal wave.

> But treated correctly, its welcome will be
> warm and gracious, allowing its full
> amusement to be absorbed.

It can be harsh, and can use force, till
one is perished in the almighty perils of the sea.

> But why? What does it hope to achieve
> 'eating the earth away'? How can it
> have a true destiny if it will be around
> for eternity?

Jon Truby (13)
Astley High School

FLUFFY LITTLE BEAR

A white and fluffy little bear,
Moved in with me last week,
I'm sure I had not invited him,
It was a bit of a cheek!

He had come down from the Arctic,
Where the weather's very cold,
And as I talked to him,
His sorry story did unfold,

You see he was a little bear,
Not very strong at that,
The unemployment rate is high,
For bears as small as that,

He couldn't fight, he couldn't fish,
He could hunt in packs,
And, worst of all, he couldn't pay,
The North Pole's Council Tax,

And so he came to my house,
And joined my family,
I hope his friends don't turn up,
'Cos there won't be room for me!

Emma Brown (15)
Astley High School

HOPE

We are all born equal
Or so they say,
But I am not equal
In so many ways.
No bread on the table
No water to drink,
And death it awaits me
Out there on the brink.
No future to plan for,
No hope just dismay,
And the pain in my stomach
Just won't go away.
The clothes I am wearing
Aren't clothes but old rags,
There's no designer's name
On my tags.
We are all born equal,
Well I don't agree
For out there there's millions
As helpless as me.
So if you've bread on your table
And water to drink,
Don't take it for granted
Just stop and think.
If you give just a little,
Whatever you can,
You could help a small boy
Grow into a man.

Nicola Waite (15)
Astley High School

PAINT MAN

The colours of love flow through your mind;
Relax a while, let your thoughts unwind.
Paint a picture inside your head,
In the rustic veins of your brain so red.

Your eyes are the easel, your soul the brush,
Your hand is steady, you're not one to rush.
You walk upon the canvas of the Earth,
Unto its pale image, you give birth.

Splashes of sunlight shine on every stroke;
Open your doors and unveil your cloak.
Wash away the black and the blue;
Your style senses the change in hue.

When you're done, leave it to dry.
Take a look and get real high.
Sign your soul upon the ground;
It's a priceless piece, pound-for-pound.

Hang it up in a hall of mirrors.
Show it to those who don't understand.
Get criticised, be paralysed.
Tear it down with bare bleeding hands.

And then you lock yourself away,
Into the depths of moral decay.
You're hidden from view, for none to see,
With only your paintings, your brush and me.

Ross Armstrong (17)
Astley High School

THIS ROOM

This room, so silent
I sit here alone
In this solitary classroom
All on my own.

Death-like, the silence crawls in
Only a crying groan
From the weeping corridors
And the children outside
Can disturb my vacant mood.

This room feels so empty
Soon to be filled
By talkative pupils
My thoughts shatter as they are killed.

Jill Fitch (15)
Astley High School

THE GERBIL AND THE CAT

Agile, little gerbil,
Evil, green eyes,
Quick, sudden pounce,
Fleeting, panicked, struggle
Satisfied, happy cat.

Chris Muir (13)
Burnside Community High School

SPELLBOUND

Witches and wizards
Warlocks and trolls
All come out under the stars.

Thin as sticks
Fat as trees
They all come out with knobbly knees

Long thin broomsticks
Big fat cats.
Big pointy noses,
Just like their hats.

They sing around a big, hot fire
Drinking blood from a tiger.
They eat the guts of little kittens
Auntie Mildred must watch her little mittens.

As the sun comes up, away they go
Away to where, nobody knows
Until the next night
With a frightful bite
Away goes a kitten in a fright.

Paul Thompson (14)
Burnside Community High School

WITCHES' SCHOOL

Cauldron burns and fire bubbles.
Over the hills where the trouble struggles,
Time for school, the witches say,
Maths and humanities we've got today.

Cauldron burns and fire bubbles,
Over the hills where the trouble struggles,
Games and science, they say tomorrow,
What about our teacher Mr Ronald.

Cauldron burns and fire bubbles,
Over the hills where the trouble struggles,
Music was played at lunchtime today,
While the young witches went out to play.

Cauldron burns and fire bubbles,
Over the hills where the trouble struggles,
Time to go home, the witches say,
I've got homework, ten bits today.

Christopher Beadle (13)
Burnside Community High School

OUTSIDE

Outside I see a thrilling view,
It was put there for me and you.
It seems to have a loving touch,
We want to see it Oh, so much.

I see a glimpse of sun shine through,
The sparkling raindrops in the morning dew.
The grass clean-cut, it smells so sweet,
I'd love to touch with my hands and feet.

The flowers swaying in the wind,
All tightly packed as if they were tinned.
The flower petals all brightly sprung,
The wind comes rushing and the pollen is flung.

As I listen to the birds outside,
I swing back the curtains and see them glide,
Their wings are feathered soft and dull
The clouds in the sky make it all look full.

David Martin (13)
Burnside Community High School

THE SEA TROUT RIVER

Looking through the hanging trees,
on my mighty river.
The fast flowing runs, the rocky lies,
the deep dark never-ending pools.
Casting across it is such a delight
in the blackness of the night.
Will I catch one of these silver
beauties, or will it continue up to do
its duty.
They take the run I may never
see, if these mighty fish keep
hiding from me.

Time is passing too quickly for me,
as are the sea trout swimming free.

Ross McRae (13)
Burnside Community High School

IF I WERE?

If I were a tree, I'd sing diddly-dee
If I were a shoe, I'd smell like you
If I were a comb, I'd run through your hair
If I were a monster, I'd be a real scare
If I were a candle, I'd be a light
If I were blind, I'd have no sight
If I were a bird, I'd fly in the sky
If I were hungry, I'd eat an apple pie
If I weren't me?

Karl Ford (13)
Burnside Community High School

FREEDOM

Galloping along,
Free and wild,
Not a care in the world
Then trapped!
Alone.

Tangled in vines,
And up-growing roots,
Lost and scared in the woods,
As a silent darkness
Hit.

I could feel his terror,
His hurt, his sorrow.
His neigh cried out across the land
For something to come
And help.

He had fear in his eyes
And hope in his heart.
He pulled and tore
With all his might
He believed.

As he pulled himself free,
His eyes filled with joy,
As he galloped and leaped
Under the moonlit sky.
Free.

Gemma Stevens (12)
High Farm Middle School

MY NANNA'S DEATH

S he was so poorly at home in bed,
A nd finding it hard to breathe.
D own in the sitting room I cried and cried, but could not stop crying.
N ow my heart is broken forever,
E ach time I think of her
S ometimes I think of the pain she was in.
S he was very special to me and I was special to her.

David Fletcher (12)
High Farm Middle School

FLAMING PREDATOR

A sharp glance burning flames
In his eyes
He stalks proudly
A conqueror in catching prey
A predator on a white-hot trail
Immeasurable in size, powerful in body
A life is finished, another one to go
As another hungry beast lingers on
An uncontrolled mind of danger
A swish of a tail like flames
His paws with claws like nails
Camouflaged, he gently creeps
His mouth scorching and spitting.
He rests like a burnt-out fire
Waiting for another release.

Ashleigh Halliburton (12)
High Farm Middle School

FIRE

Deadly so dangerous it leaps about
As hot as the sun on a mid-summer's day.
It smoulders and smokes until it breaks out
And so it crackles on its way.

Glowing in the black, black night
It shimmers in the wind.
It gives you such an awful fright
And on the wall it's pinned.

Leaping, jumping, swaying,
For all the crowd to see.
People hear you saying
'Help me Oh please help me.'

Alexis Hindhaugh (13)
High Farm Middle School

SURVIVAL

Strong waves crash onto the rock.
Smashing everything in their path
Angry they leap.
Crushing life from tiny creatures.
Flinging stones up into the air.

And on this rock a man is clinging
Desperately hanging on for his right to survive
As he is thrown, side to side
A twisted, torn and battered body.

A life may end, but another will survive.

Suezanne Foster (12)
High Farm Middle School

NEVER-ENDING NIGHT

The darkness crept upon the land,
It gripped the light of day.
The wind rampaged through the silent streets,
It was a flood of darkness.

The eye can't see,
What the ear can hear
There is a wail from out at sea,
An oasis of light shone through the cloud of darkness.

The black turned to grey and started to fracture,
It cracked all over and split down the middle.
The glittering gleam from the dazzling light,
It broke its way through with a bright white beam.

The darkness roared and fought with anger,
It pulled itself together.
Ripping through the beam of hope,
It is the master of all.

Neal Heathcote (12)
High Farm Middle School

BABE THE SHEEP-PIG

The pig in the barn stared out at the sky.
He wondered what the stars were called and why.
He dreamt of dreams he'd never dreamt before.
He had more life than the world had but still he wanted more.
He wanted something, even more than the hedgehog.
His ambition was to be a sheepdog.

Kayleigh Prescott (11)
High Farm Middle School

PARADISE

Empty beach,
Burning sands,
Palm trees cover,
Drifting lands.

Dolphins swim,
In clear seas,
The gentle buzz,
Of honey bees.

Graceful birds,
Vanish by,
Lonely sun,
In a cloudless sky.

Not a soul,
To breathe the air,
Perfect silence,

No one there . . .

Katie Askew (12)
High Farm Middle School

THE SNOWMAN

The snow is falling
Even the snowman has to
Wear a hat and scarf.

Marc Parker (12)
High Farm Middle School

THE MAGIC BOX

I will put in the box

The light of the sun
A tree from the forest
A fourteenth month
The head of a shark.

I will put in the box

The constellation of Sagittarius
A flying lighthouse
A magic bus stop
The musical brain of Mrs Trodden

I will put in the box

The force of gravity
The speck of dust on my shoe
My liking of recording playing
This ink from my pen to my paper

I will put in the box

The comet flying through the sky
The love of my parents
The spirit of my Grandma
And the love I gave her.

My box is made of solid gold
Because of the light of the sun
With a golden eagle on top.
It has my name carved on the back.

Claire Hope (11)
High Farm Middle School

THE NIGHT MAN

The night man prances,
Through the night.
He'll fill you full of,
Shock and fright,.
While you're sleeping,
In your bed.
Listen for,
He'll lightly tread
Through the corridor,
And up the stair.
With almost the slightest,
Bit of care.
Because if someone was to,
Catch him and
Grab him by his ghostly hand,
He would simply run away,
And disappear into another day.
Because his magic is as,
Dark and black,
As a ghost train,
Running along a track.
So if you see him,
Running free,
Just pretend,
You didn't see.

Toni Ford (12)
High Farm Middle School

PASSION FRUIT PINK

Long stick legs
Paddling through the waters
Pink feathers everywhere
On its soft body
Carefully using its beak
Catching fish
On the muddy banks.
A flamingo
A slim bright pink flamingo
Her body large
Her wing-span huge
Her slim legs massive
All this is the flamingo
A slim, bright pink flamingo
Far, far away.

Nicola Goudie (12)
High Farm Middle School

A DRAGON

A dragon is a fierce beast
Always looking for a feast
The flying fireball approaches a town
Spits some fire and then swoops down
For now it's time for the red beast's meal
Of toasted chops and roasted veal.
The cunning giant is harpooned out the sky
Down he falls ready to die
He's chained to the ground and wound, wound, wound
Around with string, so he can't move a thing
For now it's the end of the dragon's life
Brought to death by a thrust of a knife.

Ben Macauley (12)
High Farm Middle School

SPITFIRE

Soaring through the vast
blue sky.
Pilots knowing the time of
death is nigh.

The outline of the Luftwaffe
is up ahead.
Our gallant men may soon
be dead.

The German bombers draw
ever near.
But our swift Spitfires
they do fear.

On the attack the Spitfire
dives.
The Luftwaffe in devastation
the Royal Airforce has thrived.

The Spitfire does a roll in glory.
The spoils of war are dull and gory.

Andrew Mills (12)
High Farm Middle School

ACCIDENTS IN SCHOOL

A chopped-off finger in CDT
A boy in 5th year with a scratched knee
In the science lab there's a big bang
Oh no, in the music room, Miss Jones sang
Fell off the box top in PE.
There's a fight in the play-yard can't you see?
In HE there's a cake on the floor
Then a teacher came through the door
It was a complete and utter disaster
The room was full of joy and laughter
In English the drama was a mess
But what is worse you wouldn't guess
The head teacher said 'You in the corner'
The girl turned red like she'd been in a sauna
Some pupils were caught with chewing gum
Then Peter Smith got stuck on a sum
When the bell rang they went with a zoom
Then the caretaker fell over his broom!

Laura Clelland (12)
High Farm Middle School

STORM

An horrific storm commences,
The rain lashes down,
On the earth below,
Deeply drenching its population.

Is this a demon?

Thor is furious,
Punishing mankind.
Each blinding flash of light,
Closely followed by a
Terrorising roar of thunder.

Do we deserve this?

A blustery wind overpowers man,
It is the master,
And we are its slave.
The cold, cruel sky above,
All grey and gloomy.
Hides the sun behind its
Thick, bitter, black curtain of cloud.
This devilish evil spell is infinite.

Will this nightmare end . . .?

Helen Blowers (12)
High Farm Middle School

FRUITS

Colourful fruits sweet and nutritious
I'd rather eat them than do the dishes
Apples, oranges, pears and kiwi
All of these are appetisingly juicy
Some can be bright and some can be dull
But then there's the spiky pineapple
They can be sweet, exotic and tangy
Vivid, gay and also gaudy
Bright and sour is the lemon
Apples are green and crimson
A big fruity bubble ready to burst
Oranges can really quench your thirst
Fruits are healthy and good for you too
So make sure you put them on your menu.

Carly Smith (12)
High Farm Middle School

THE DARKNESS

The darkness of the night,
Is soft, welcoming, exhilarating.
It feels so different,
So separate from the day,
That on a clear night,
When the stars shine,
Can be felt a unique freedom,
Born of the dark,
Unknown to the day.

Catriona Rutherford (13)
Marden High School

IF ONLY . . .

I close the door behind me,
Shutting out the world,
Yet this feeling is still lingering in my head.

I cannot change the past,
It's far too late to try.
But self-hatred is still nagging at my heart.

I wish I hadn't done it.

I cry into my pillow.
Knowing it won't help.
I try, but my tears won't cease to flow.

The dread seeps through my body,
Drowning rational thought.
As I curse myself and hope I can forget.

I wish I hadn't done it.

I had the opportunity.
I threw away my chance.
It would have been so easy to say no.

As time rolls by I contemplate,
What life could have been like.
That day changed me forever. What a waste.

I wish I hadn't done it,
But I did.

Helen Lockey (15)
Marden High School

UGLY DUCKLING SUICIDE

We found her on the beach
a contented smile making
her face beautiful.
As icy waves lapped
at her blue toes,
she looked like an angel
her white dress spread
about her like wings.
Every day that we saw
her painted, unnatural
face,
we sniggered, thinking
she would never be
attractive.
Lying on the beach
her lifeless form was
the most beautiful
we had ever seen.

Kate Hudson (15)
Marden High School

NIGHTFALL

Watching the night close in,
The moving shadows across the wall,
The hidden secrets open up;
The fear, the loneliness of the dark.

Magic celebrations come alive
As witchcraft dawns another night,
Waiting to devastate earthly nature,
Controlling the blanket of silence.

Wicked dreams abuse the mind,
Exaggerated imagery forms inside
Conjuring up an unsightly picture;
The fear, the loneliness of the dark.

As dawn swallows the thick night,
Reality drives the mind again,
Returning the bright innocent day
To force fear and loneliness away.

Elin Wallis (15)
Marden High School

NIGGER

'Nigger, nigger!' chanted the bullies
As the black girl cried.

She felt alone
It was 10 against 1.
She was afraid.

'Go back where you came from!' yelled one of the gang.

'Why should I!' she sobbed.
The tears poured down her face.
They made her skin go blotchy.
She wished she was a magician,
So she could disappear.

In the distance she could hear the bell
Which meant break was over,
But home time was still to come,
They would attack her again.

Vicky Ellison (13)
Marden High School

Is This Really A Life?

Standing alone, no one to talk to.
Does anyone care?
A mind trapped in a painful experience.
A child full of laughter,
The days are long gone.
Trapped in a world,
Too afraid to speak out.
What will it be this time?
Money?
Food?
Laughter?

Black and blue.
Limbs broken.
Kicked and punched all over.
The mental scars are what remain,
The cruel taunts and laughter
Why me? Cries a voice. Why me?
No one has any answers.

A victim suffering in silence.
The pain of living in fear.
Taunted.
Miserable.
Is this really a life?
Stand up for yourself.
Stand up for yourself tall and strong.
It's not that easy when there's more than one.
Not confident enough?
Not strong enough to win?

Bullies are cowards.
Afraid of individuals.
Frightened of what they'll do.
They want authority over their innocent victims . . .
But if they stand up for themselves -
Show they're not afraid,
And don't let them win,
Only then the nightmare will be reversed . . .
And they'll be afraid of you.

Nicola Gordon (15)
Marden High School

SWIMMING NOWHERE

I swim through my life like a fish in the sea,
Going nowhere, wanting nothing . . .
But now I've hit a shipwreck,
I don't know what to do.
I don't know where to go . . .

Because everywhere I turn is a tangled mess of weed.

So I carry on swimming,
But I don't know where I'm going . . .

I'm not going anywhere

Nowhere fast.

Fiona O'Keefe (15)
Marden High School

FEAR

Are you afraid?
Do you wish the light had stayed?
Blackness folds over your eyes,
Dancing shadows, terror lies
Fear for your sanity's life
Taunting spirit, gleaming knife

Are you afraid?
Would you like to live a million days?
Some of us fear our mortality,
Others await the embrace of fatality.
Those whose lives are pleasure-kissed
Know not, oblivion lies in your warm, red, wrist.

Are you still afraid?
The roads of fear have all been laid
Do you want me to stop?
They all wait for you to walk atop.
Sweating palm, bleary, bloodshot eyes,
No sleep for you, till fear will die.

Do you think it will . . .?

Keith Patterson (16)
Marden High School

IMAGINE
(Every year 450,000 calves, 2,000,000 sheep and 70,000 pigs
are exported from Britain to Europe)

Imagine the darkness closing in,
Not a light to be seen.
Imagine the solitary, the loneliness,
As if in another world.

Imagine not being able to turn around,
Not even able to lie down.
Imagine being starved to death,
Driven crazy by thirst.

Imagine being beaten, kicked, punched,
Your legs broken for no reason.
Imagine being dragged by your ears,
Because you were too weak to move.

Imagine dying of suffocation,
Or being trampled to death.
Imagine dying of fear,
Fifty hours of hell.

Imagine if this was you,
Travelling to your death.

Emma Murray (15)
Marden High School

THE STAIRCASE OF LIFE

Do not grieve over me.
Do not spend eternal nights weeping into the darkness.
I am merely one step ahead on the fabric of time.
For death is only one more step up the staircase of life.

Do not spend lonesome evenings with sad memories.
Do not dwell in the past.
I am only around the corner of existence.
For death is only one more step up the staircase of life.

Do not forget the happy times.
Do not forget me.
I am merely in another room.
For death is only one more step up the staircase of life.

Do not drown other friends in your sorrows.
Do not cry over my disappearance.
Life is a terminal illness.
For death is only one more step up the staircase of life.

Catriona Atkinson (15)
Marden High School

AUTUMN DAYS

Autumn leaves fluttering and blowing around
before they fall upon the cold, cold ground,
they skip and dance and jump and run
under the chilly autumn sun.

The bright red berries soon begin to drop
from the holly bushes, bottom, middle and top.
The squirrels eat all of the best
before they go for their long winter's rest.

We people stay inside all warm and snug
trying not to catch a cold or the flu bug.
When the cold nights draw in,
you shut your curtains and stay within.

The birds fly to southern land
for a warm climate is what they demand.
I love this season every time it comes,
How I long for the autumn.

Andrea Dietz (11)
St Anthony's Girls' School

HAMSTERS

H airy, fluffy, furry,
A lways asleep during the day.
M oving rapidly round the cage at night.
S oft padded paws.
T ail short and stumpy.
E ars always listening for danger.
R eally smelly sometimes.
S hort fat furry bodies.

Nicola James (12)
St Anthony's Girls' School

SEASONS

On the ground thick layers of snow,
Cold biting winds strongly do blow,
Frost-covered trees without their leaves,
And the birds flew south long ago,
And the birds flew south long ago.

The rain patters on the ground,
And buds form on the trees,
Newborn lambs are in the fields,
Among green shoots, flowers and leaves,
Among green shoots, flowers and leaves.

The blue sky is perfectly clear
But for the sun that strongly beats down,
Bright flowers fair are everywhere,
And pure happiness is easily found,
And pure happiness is easily found.

Fields of corn - yellow and poppies - red,
Are waiting for harvest to come,
The colourful leaves, fallen from trees,
Are filling the earth with colour,
Are filling the earth with colour.

Clare Ricketts (11)
St Anthony's Girls' School

LIFE'S JOURNEY

Life is a journey.
Like a train on a track.
Over the hills and then right back.
Like sudden memories you retrace your tracks.
Over the hills and then right back.

There is a mountain bigger than ever
you have to climb it no matter the weather.

The mountain is anger, the mountain is pain,
over it you go then right back again.
The mountain is achievement the
mountain is success
Once you've got it, it's easy all the rest.

Samantha Spraggon (11)
St Anthony's Girls' School

DISASTER GRANNY

Granny came to stay one day,
Her face was covered with wrinkles her hair was
Tattered and grey.

She sat down to eat,
But my brother knocked her off her feet.

As she began to shout,
Her false teeth fell out.

She went to pick them up,
And smashed a cup.

She walked away with her head up,
And cut her leg on the cup.

Laura Conlon (11)
St Anthony's Girls' School

WHAT ON EARTH?

Who thought
of animals?
Really big and small.
In fact,
Why are they there at all?
Who made the earth?
Really big and round,
and why doesn't it
rest upon the ground?

Are there really ghosts
Right upon this earth?
Regarding hyenas,
what's the cause of their mirth?

Who invented blu-tack
and why are misers mean?
And most of all I
wonder
why the
grass is green?
What are the saints?
And how come they're no more?
What is a real friend?
And why obey the law?

Lindsey Bell (11)
St Anthony's Girls' School

OLD PEOPLE

Old people and their past life,
Can often be forgot.
Their lively childhood memories,
Left in minds to rot.

Why do we just forget them,
And get on with our youth,
If we just listen to their voice,
They really know the truth.

Soon, they fall in a deep sleep,
And then placed in the ground,
They stay there very peacefully,
They lie there safe and sound.

And then do people realise,
How we forget them so,
They then begin to notice,
They are who made us grow.

Next time just take some notice,
Of what they have to say,
Because they're brilliant people,
Till their dying day!

Helen Wilson (11)
St Anthony's Girls' School

ADULT SUPERVISION

'Put that away'
'Tidy that desk'
I'm sick of hearing that.

'Do your homework'
'Turn that music down'
I hear that all the time.

'Do you know what time it is?'
'Get to bed'
Ah, I'm getting a headache now!

'Wake up'
'Put your uniform on'
Oh no.

'Wash that dish'
'Make that bed'
Does this torture ever end?

Laura Kelly (11)
St Anthony's Girls' School

REX

My house is bigger than your house.
My car's better than your car.
My dad's tougher than your dad,
And my pet's better than yours.
I wouldn't let Rex hear you say that,
I am not scared.
Are you sure, you see,
When I say Rex I mean
T-Rex and he's standing next to you!

Katie Roddy (11)
St Anthony's Girls' School

BLACK AS NIGHT

It is so quiet
And so still
Makes you want to jump
Gives you a chill.

When lying in bed
Still as the grave
You are sure you hear voices
In that big black cave.

As you see the clock you
See the witching hour is nigh
And you see
No stars in that black winter's sky.

Eerie and frightening
You wish someone
Would listen
And you hear thunder and lightning
Ooh frightening.

Laura Gulliver (11)
St Anthony's Girls' School

ALIENS

Aliens are creatures
from outer-space.
Lonely little people
who walk a slow pace.

Is it that green colour,
that makes them so queer?
Either that or, it's because
they come from Tyne & Wear.

Cristina Nethercott (11)
St Anthony's Girls' School

TREE OF MYSTERY

Trees, trees are everywhere
        sometimes full, sometimes bare.
Starting off ever so small
        they grow and grow oh so tall.

While the seed is in the ground
        you can search but it won't be found.
After time some shoots appear
        but still its future isn't clear.

There's so many trees it could be
        but we'll just have to wait and see!
Through the seasons and many a year
        different changes will occur.

With its branches fully grown
        the mystery of the tree was known.
The little red fruit that I could see
        meant it could only be a cherry tree.

Claire Maughan (11)
St Anthony's Girls' School

IF I COULD FLY

If I had wings, such beautiful wings
The kind the phoenix had,
I'd ascend high, and see the sky
Then plummet down to earth.

From up above the human beings
Look just like tiny ants,
And the giant Amazon rainforest
Looks like a single plant.

And over there in Egypt
Where the Toblerones stand still,
As the Nile flows past so tranquilly
Like sails on a windmill.

Now as I descend back to earth
I study the idyllic scene
As I know that there will never be
Another chance to fly again.

Jennifer Bayley (11)
St Anthony's Girls' School

MY FAMILY IS BETTER THAN YOURS

My mam is better than your mam
she takes me to all the fairs.
My mam is better than your mam
she buys me teddy bears.

My brother is better than your brother
he lets me in his room.
My brother is better than your brother
he promised me a trip to the moon.

My sister is better than your sister
she takes me in all the shops.
My sister is better than your sister
she buys me lollipops.

My dad is better than your dad
he drives me to and from school.
My dad is better than your dad
because he only has one rule
and that's
My family is better than yours!

Zoe Greenfield (11)
St Anthony's Girls' School

IT WASN'T AS BAD AS I THOUGHT

There he stands in coat of white,
Me wishing I could have a flight
Away.

Checking if everything is clean,
He comes over looking pristine
Towards me.

He glances at his sinister tools,
Wondering which he would have to use
On me.

After choosing with what to torture,
Approaches to begin the slaughter.
I freeze.

After all the fuss it wasn't that bad,
For my tooth had been driving me mad
Last night.

When it's done and finally all over,
I remark to my brother,
'You're next.'

Then he turns a shade of green,
Something which I have never seen
Before.

Except this morning looking in the mirror,
When I caught sight of my fear of visiting
The dentist!

Catherine Taroni (11)
St Anthony's Girls' School

WEEKENDS

S aturdays are fab,
A nd they're fantastic,
T uesdays are boring and glum,
U nique Saturdays are the best,
R eady for Saturdays there's no doubt about that,
D ancing and shopping are hobbies for Saturday
A nd of course watching TV.
Y ep Saturdays are great
S o go ahead and enjoy yours!

S undays are okay I suppose
U nder my quilt I snuggle up.
'N ow Mitra get up this instant!'
'D on't want to be late for church'
A ctually Sundays are quite good,
Y es I look forward to Sundays,
S o that makes weekends fab!

Mitra Akrami (11)
St Anthony's Girls' School

SPOOKY

S pine-chilling howls and a mysterious creak,
P rowling wolves start to sneak,
O ut of the door and into the wood,
O n an old tree stump silently stood
K ing of the vampires now under a tree
Y ellow haze begins to rise, just as he begins to flee.

Emma J Matthews (11)
St Anthony's Girls' School

SEASONS

S pring approaches as slow as a snail
P erhaps a flower waits to greet her
R unning, playing in the garden
I leap high like a frog
N othing moves, only me
G oing from flower to flower like a bee.

S ummer comes with its bright sun
U nder its brightness, I can see
M illions of flowers spring has left behind
M other, quick come see the view
E verybody, so can you!
R ain clouds go away come again another day.

A utumn brings the reds and browns
U nderneath the bare tree branches
T urns the ground into a great oil painting
U gly now, the tree may look
M any people admire the colour
N ow like a picture in a book.

W inter comes with its icy chill
I n the late months of the year
N o more flowers can be seen
T hrough the fields, no more green.
E very child playing in the snow
R udolf and Santa here we go . . .

Helen Thompson (11)
St Anthony's Girls' School

1984

1984 was the year I was born,
Brighton bombing families all began to mourn.
Yvonne Fletcher the policewoman was also killed,
Torvill and Dean's dreams of winning Gold fulfilled.

Prince Harry was born on the 15th of September,
Demise of the pound note on the 12th of November.
Desmond Tutu wins the Nobel Peace Prize,
Miners go on strike over Tory lies.

A Sikh assassin ends Mrs Gandhi's life,
Elton John on Valentine's Day takes a wife.
A lightning strike burns York Minster roof,
The Peat Marsh man reveals the ancient truth.

Just a few events the year '84 brought,
Looking back on this time lessons are taught.
A baby Rebecca was born in this year,
Just one of the events that caused quite a stir.

Rebecca Atkinson (13)
St Anthony's Girls' School

WINTER

It's cold it's damp,
It's misty and muggy,
The trees are nearly bare,
The air is still.
Not a sound to be heard,
Oh where is the singing from birds,
I look all around me,
Everything looks
Dull and grey.
Then I remember,
It's a winter's day.

Joanna Kerr (11)
St Anthony's Girls' School

THE TEST

It points to him,
No not him,
He's not ready, but it's too late,
He's written his name and the date,
He slips on the first question,
. . . And the next,
He's almost destroyed,
Verdict *F*.
But then bright kid's turn name and date,
First question right and the next one
Great.
The paper explodes in a fit of rage,
But believe me it will return to fight another day,
Verdict *A*.

Adam Clery (10)
St Mary's RC Primary School

FIVE HEARTS

When I was young,
My heart was full of adventure,
I went to the sun and back,
Underneath me dragons and pirates.

When I was growing up,
My heart was full of dreams,
I circled the world,
A river of happiness flowed by.

When I was grown,
My heart was full of love,
It was like a bridge joining two people,
Making me happy,
Keeping me from pain.

When I was old,
My heart was full of fear and memories,
I trusted no one,
I kept myself to myself,
For thinking people would call me a fool.

Now I am dying,
My heart is full of hope,
A silver light shines on my place in Heaven.

Laura Richards (9)
St Mary's RC Primary School

CLASSROOM CAPERS

It was just an ordinary day
when my pencil started to sway.
First it lifted in the air,
trying its best to hold itself there.
Sophie screamed 'Look over there,
The chalk is moving in the air.'
We looked, we saw, it couldn't be true.
For there, in front of us, out of the blue
the chalk was writing on the board.
We all sat there totally absorbed
in what the chalk had started writing.
It was a most peculiar sighting.
The chalk stopped suddenly and broke in two.
Children ran into the loo.
Zoë turned white, Emma fainted,
and all the things we had painted
fell onto the dusty classroom floor.
Moving people ran out of the door.
Only me, Amy and Phillip stayed.
Then ghostly music suddenly played.
A shadowy figure now appeared,
so 'scaredy-cat' Phillip disappeared.
The ghostly sight said, 'Yoo hoo'
Amy asked, 'Who are you?'
'I am Mary' the spectre said,
'And I am unfortunately very dead.
I wish to know the date.'
I thought *hurry up, this ghost won't wait.*
I looked at her with hidden dismay,
for it was Friday the 13th today!

Rebecca Younger (10)
St Mary's RC Primary School

WHAT MAKES ME HAPPY

'Rise up, rise up,'
said the clouds to the sun,
'from you' the clouds said, 'all good things come.
Children dance and smile and sing,
and you my friend can feel like a king.
All the good things you have done,
can be shared with everyone.
So please, O please, please come out,
to hear the children sing and shout.'
The sun said, 'I'll take a peep,
but if I don't like it, I'll go back to sleep.'
The sun rose up from his nest,
from his very tiring rest.
The sun stretched up and took a yawn,
to find that it was only dawn.
The sun shone bright, from dawn till night,
then the sun went and the moon was sent.
The moon tonight was awfully slow,
so when he got there, it began to snow.
It happened all through the night,
then in the morning with all his might,   and away
the sun burst out and with a shout,   up
he melted the snow,   up
And pulled it up

Amy Wright (9)
St Mary's RC Primary School

THE SEA

Storm
Whirling like a cyclone in my mind
Angry cruel sea
Crashing waves
Foaming spray
Hurricane
Lashing, smashing,
Thrashing, crashing,
Splashing
All the way

Sea
Peaceful and placid
Quiet and cool
Chameleon colours
Azure, sapphire
Cyan, emerald
Fresh breeze
Rippling the restful waves.

Katherine O'Connor (10)
St Mary's RC Primary School

DREAMS

Running through the clouds,
Meeting everyone you see
The strong wind blowing in your face
It starts at the crack of dawn
And vanishes at sunset
You can hear the wild dogs calling
When the sunset falls.
I wake up.

Laura Doyle (8)
St Mary's RC Primary School

I WANT A STAR

'Stars they're so bright, but they're up -
so high,' my mother said to me.
'But I want a star,' I said, and I started to cry,
She said 'Why don't you splash in a puddle?
Or I will get you a teddy to cuddle.'
'But I want a star, I want a star,
I want a star!'
So I kept on wailing until she got me one.
But I was looking in the sky and I saw
the moon, and I said, 'I want the moon!'

Shannon Francis Dalton (9)
St Mary's RC Primary School

THE FOX

The fox is tunnelling underground.
It is ready for a sleep.
It's tired after chasing rabbits.
Red tail swaying as it scrapes mud away.
The pointed ears listening out for voices and footsteps.

Francesca Croft (8)
St Mary's RC Primary School

FISH

I saw a fish swimming in the sea.
Fish are friends to me.
They are nice the fish in the sea.
They have mums and dads just like me.

Lucy Summers (6)
St Mary's RC Primary School

THE HAPPIEST DAY

On the saddest day, yes it may have to come,
Everyone will fight, swear, argue and have no fun.
So then we'll find we don't like it that way, so we ask
Our friends to come out and play.
And on the happiest day, everyone will laugh, dance and
Sing, not fighting, arguing or doing such a thing.
There won't be a tear in anyone's eye, just a smile to lighten
Up the sky.
So don't have sadness, don't have fear, and let the
Happiest day be here.
So that someone can laugh,
Someone can smile,
And someone can have freedom for the very first time.

Kelly Knight (9)
St Mary's RC Primary School

THE DIARY

Mary had a diary,
A very secret diary,
She used to write in it all day,
And never used to play.
Her dad said she was nutty,
Her brother said to play footy
And her mother said to eat putty.
Mary didn't listen to a single thing said,
She just closed her diary and went to bed.

Ciar McGoldrick (8)
St Mary's RC Primary School

THE CAR WASH

We were being abducted by aliens,
I just knew it
The car was covered in white
. . . with something that looked like snow
We couldn't see anything
I panicked
Mum and Dad didn't look too worried though
Two pillar-shaped objects tried to squash me
My car came to the rescue
It dealt with them swiftly - they left
We were out
I wanted to shout
I wanted to see the alien spaceship
. . . so I gingerly looked behind
I wanted to laugh of course . . .
It was only the car wash
Oops!

Josh Kenolty (10)
St Mary's RC Primary School

MY NATURE POEM

Chestnut, ginger and chocolate brown.
Falling off the bright green trees.
Scarlet, cherry and foxy red.
Hard and inflexible, smooth and flat.
Dark and rosy, bumpy and firm.
Rigid and rocky, cool and fresh.
Bright, yellow and golden blonde.
Conkers fallen on the ground.

Beth Hetherington (8)
St Mary's RC Primary School

AUTUMN LEAVES

Golden nut and golden leaves fall off trees one by one,
Crispy noises can be heard from all those crispy leaves,
A hazel colour can be seen in the distance.
You come closer and closer and all it is is a hazel brown
chestnut on the floor.
Barbs are there near it and crushy leaves are next to it.
Run and run and all you can hear is your feet on those
leaves, *crush crush crush.*
You're trying to touch every crusty leaf.
Spiky things are on the floor.
And you fall.
It's close, you fell on the leaves and not the spiky things.
You hear a *crush crush crush.*
And that's the wind blowing the crispy crunchy leaves,
Off the floor
And they land on you and you stand back up and
you run back home.
But you can still hear your own two feet on the floor.
Crush crush crush.

Martha Seif (8)
St Mary's RC Primary School

GOING TO THE SHOPS

Have I got the keys?
Have I got my purse?
Have I got my coat?
Have I switched the lights off?
Have I shut the door?
Yes I've got everything
Now let's spend some money.

Matthew Moore (6)
St Mary's RC Primary School

MY KEEPING BUSY BOOK

In my keeping busy book, it's where I spend my time.
It's where I'm busy when I'm bored,
It's where I'm happy when I'm sad,
It's where I'm brave when I'm scared,
'Cos all I have to do is flick it through.
In my keeping busy book, it's where I always write.
It's where I write what I do,
And count up my merits which happen to be in there too,
I read about countries and capitals,
And see shapes made from circles.
I practise in here all the time.
I am even writing this poem in here first.
The only problem with my keeping busy book,
Is that half of it is blank!

Claire Moore (9)
St Mary's RC Primary School

STARS

Stars are bright
they shine their light
every night high up in the sky.
The stars shine down on me
I make a wish
upon the brightest star I see
in the sky at night.
Stars stars so bright up there
I wish I was a star
to shine all night in that funny shape.

Finn McGoldrick (10)
St Mary's RC Primary School

THE SKY

The stars are fireflies dancing in the night,
The moon is a white lily shimmering in the light,
The sun is a marigold that glitters in the sky,
A rainbow is a picture that is mixed with many
different colours.
And the sky is bright blue, with white mist for the clouds.

The rain is water, trickling from a little waterfall from
a little stream,
The wind is a weird and wonderful howling giant,
The mist is a warm cool feeling,
The thunder and lightning are vicious creatures tossing
and turning in the sea.
And the sky is bright blue, with white mist for the clouds.

Zoë Hakin (10)
St Mary's RC Primary School

THE DREADED WHIRLPOOL

The water spinning,
fast and fierce, dragging anything
that comes near.
Twirling, rolling nice and wet,
in a circle, millions of miles
heading west.
Boats and sea monsters being
pulled in, as if there were a
thousand men, pulling ropes on
each of them.
Getting dizzy as we go,
and there's only one way to go.
Down. Down. *Down!*

Jonathan Lavery (10)
St Mary's RC Primary School

DOUBLE HENRY

Henry the VII was a nice young chap,
He seemed pretty nice from what I have heard,
But it seems to me,
All he did with valuable time was count
his dough and drink his wine,
But as for Henry, Henry the VIII,
He seemed to do a lot,
Besides drinking and having a son,
He did his church duty to God,
Archery and tiring horses were one of
Henry's many courses,
Now I have told you about the Tudors,
I bet you all want to be rulers!

Mhairi McMullon (9)
St Mary's RC Primary School

MY PARENTS' SMELLY FEET

Are your parents' feet smelly?
Mine are!
At night I get a fright
When my parents take their socks off!
Their feet are sweaty, it's embarrassing
When my friends come to stay.
This is because they pong all day.
So we spray the house with deodorant!

Hannah Lillford (10)
St Mary's RC Primary School

LIGHTNING

Twisting and turning like an eel's tail,
Just as fatal.
As it crashes through the dark night,
It will be one story to tell.

It flickers and twists,
To grab hold of your wrists
Like a demon lurking from hell.

Paul Scott (10)
St Mary's RC Primary School

DREAMS

Finding out you haven't revised,
the day of your exam,
Going to school naked,
covered in strawberry jam.
Dreams, what do they all mean.

Trying to run away,
but your feet are stuck on the ground,
Having the winning ticket,
You've won a million pound.
Dreams, what do they all mean.

Falling, falling through the air,
Waking before you land,
What do these dreams mean,
I'll never understand.

Marie Cross (15)
St Thomas More High School

BROKEN

If I gave you my heart
Would you break it in two?
This pain is slow and gradual
That I'm going through

Why do you not feel
The way I do?
You're making me feel
like I'm below you

If there was anything
I could do for you I would
like a mother caring for her
children in the hood.

I feel it when you hug me
that we were never meant to be
So I'm trying to let go
Believe me

Am I not supposed to feel low?
I'm low enough to cry
But there's nothing left to do

I can tell now that
you don't want me
so I'm going to let it be

The question I have asked
Has now come clear to me:
You have already broken my heart in two
or can you just not see what
you have done to me.

Elisabeth Vasey (15)
St Thomas More High School

THE GREAT WHITE SHARK

The great white shark,
Moving on the surface of the water,
Waiting for his dinner to appear,

The seal gliding in the water,
And all of a sudden there is
a big bang like an explosion
of fire

And a rip of raw flesh to appear,
The sea turns into a sea,
Of pure red blood
And the seal's head is dead!

Christopher Summerly (12)
St Thomas More High School

IS DEATH PLANNED?

I just don't understand
is death planned?
Everyone seems so plain
People say they must pass away
Can someone please explain
Why all the hurt and pain?
It happens to everyone sometime
The reason I don't really care
This feeling I have inside me
Of love I never could share.

Kirsty Renton (15)
St Thomas More High School

RUNNING FROM THE FUTURE

Standing here
In total fear
Should I go today.
I'm always getting hits
And I'm tortured to bits
I'm thinking I shouldn't stay.

I kill a 'bot
I'm feeling hot
Today is to be the day.
I get outside
Nowhere to hide
I hope I won't have to pay.

I run into a light
I see a space-bug in flight
I'm afraid today is the day.
I can see it flying
Soon I will be dying
I know today is the day.

The sirens are sounding
My heart is pounding
Now is the time of the day.
I have a shot
So does a 'bot
I have now had to pay.

Lying face down
No help around
Today is the day.
I get an implant
I can hear them chant
He is a 'bot today.

Andrew Grant (15)
St Thomas More High School

COUGHS AND COLDS

Did you know there's a little cruel man living at the
Back of my throat who builds a fire especially for me.
He lights it up at the daytime and kills it at night when
it's time for bed.
The fire has made my throat so dry and a burning that I have
never felt before.
The noises that I make, don't seem to go away the wheezing
The spluttering and the full blast fog horns that make my throat worse.
The hot sweets that I never seem to stop sucking don't seem
to do much good.
The mornings are the worst, getting out of bed with no voice
until you really wake up.
My nose never seems to stop running it's like a tap that is
always on.
The handkerchiefs I go through is amazing, handkerchiefs
are everywhere.
Then to cap it all off you are in agony with the
never-ending pins and needles in your head and
you ache all over.
This is what a cough or cold feels like,
for your sake I hope you don't get one.

Stacey Heard (15)
St Thomas More High School

FRIENDS

F riends are always there for you
R eliable and trustworthy
I know all their secrets
E veryone's happy with friends
N eed a helping hand?
D on't worry your friends are there.

Siobhan Campbell (12)
St Thomas More High School

I AM GOING TO THE MATCH

Crowds around me
People you wouldn't want to see.
All together as one.
Part of the same atmosphere
I am going to the match.

I've never been before
because I am a bit of a bore.
I am frightened I'll not get in
but I am going to the match.

I'll be there in a min
to see them put them in.
They run about a field
as I sit back and watch.

I am at the match
I am not afraid
I've overcome my fear
I think I'll do it again
but when I am full of beer.

Christopher Potts (15)
St Thomas More High School

THE BULLIES

When I get out of the house they hunt me down,
like animals pouncing out, they punch, kick
and shout at me like wild animals running free.
When I get home I know I'm weak just
a hopeless little freak. They have won and
I have lost the war but I know I will
get more tomorrow as soon as I open the door!

Sarah Taylor (12)
St Thomas More High School

SCHOOL RULES

Rules
Don't run,
Don't chew
Don't shout,

Rules
Keep quiet,
Please keep quiet.

Rules
Trainers trainers,
are you wearing trainers.

Rules
Don't run,
Don't chew,
Don't shout.

Where are you going,
You should be in class,
Rules.

Rules
Bend 'em,
Change 'em
Break 'em,
Rules.

What would it be like
Without rules.

Rules are for life,
When we're gone,
Will there still be rules.

Alex Talbot (15)
St Thomas More High School

TESTS

Tests what are they for?
Are they just to get on your nerves or to frustrate you?
Because that's how it makes me feel.
I hate tests.

No matter how long you revise,
It is never enough
You might as well throw your books away.
I hate tests.

Tests give me pains which are real in my mind.
My hands tremble like leaves on a windy day.
My palms and brow are sticky with sweat
I hate tests.

I feel like a man about to run a major race.
Or a football player before the big match.
I felt that my stomach has done a thousand somersaults.
I hate tests.

Tests are annoying
Tests are stupid
Tests are boring
I hate tests.

If we did not have tests we won't have jobs.
Without jobs we won't get money.
Tests.

Neil Sewell (15)
St Thomas More High School

CHAMPIONS LEAGUE

All us Geordies are excited been waiting
For this night since Ketsbara sunk Zagreb
We're here in the Champions League
And nothing can stop us from having
a good time.

Me and my dad get into the Irish pub
Two minutes' walk to the Toon's stadium of sound
We have a pint with our friends and
chat about the match

Time was flying
The atmosphere building up
And it's nearly time to go to the match
We look out the window as the Toon's
marching band goes past
Banging drums and the army behind
singing to the beat

We now make our short journey to
the match
Singing songs and having a laugh
Everyone happy and bubbly as the
match was moments away

We're in the ground
And the Toon comes out with
Mighty Barcelona at their side
The atmosphere was electric
And I'm losing my voice.

The Toon win the match 3-2
Against one of the strongest sides in
the world
Tino gets a hat trick and everyone going
home is chanting 'Tino Tino.'

Billy McIver (15)
St Thomas More High School

I'M NO GOOD AT FIGHTING

I throw a punch
I get the hunch
I'm no good at fighting
Although I'm big
He gives me a dig
I'm no good at fighting.

I go to kick
He's too quick
I'm no good at fighting
I'm in a fight
I'll get even tonight
But I'm no good at fighting.

He bites my ear
I run in fear
I'm no good at fighting
He may be small
Yet made me fall
I'm no good at fighting.

Who am I kidding
That I'm the world's greatest champion
I'm just no good at fighting.

He's coming in my dream
I start to scream
I'm no good at fighting
I'll beat him once and for all
I don't fool myself at all
I'm no good at fighting
I'm just no good at fighting at all.

David Henderson (15)
St Thomas More High School

LONELY

Lonely I am lonely,
I have no friends,
No one understands,
I don't understand,
Why am I lonely?
Lonely I am lonely,
Now I've understood,
To them I'm different,
I do things differently
to them,
I am so alone!

Lonely no more,
I stood up to them
bullies!

Friends we are!

Zoë Barwick (12)
St Thomas More High School

EVIL TEACHERS

Evil teachers that impound your pets in drawers.
Evil teachers that make you stay behind for laughing too much.
Torture devices on their desk in disguise as crocodile type
Staple removers, and large brown holdalls to carry away the evidence.
Piles of books staring out threats
Evil staring eyes mounted on wall
The inviting distant light of escaping school and looking for work.
School is the first sentence of life and probably the worst.

Jonathan Parr (15)
St Thomas More High School

HURT

Betrayed for the first time,
The pain is indescribable,
But through the pain comes anger,
The hurt slips away,
The anger rages,
I won't forgive, why should I?
How could he?
He said he loved us,
But how could that be?
He knows he hurt,
More than just me.
I won't forgive, why should I?
Through the rage,
The hurt comes back.
I still love him,
But pride won't step back,
I won't forgive, why should I?
My stomach swirls,
My heart aches,
I'm empty,
Not with material things,
But with the feelings I've lost,
There's something missing,
But I won't forgive, what's the point?

Michelle McBeth (15)
St Thomas More High School

MARK

He had a dry sense of humour, a certain kind of wit
the only person I knew that had.
My aunties said that I was so much like him
When he was my age, but how could that be,
I was just a lad!
When he first heard the terrible news,
He must of thought he wouldn't live,
With all the treatment his body refused,
I wondered what help I could give?

He was so brave, his parents too,
All of the pain they must of went through,
To lose his leg at such a young age,
What could I do to stop his rage?

I was too young to really understand,
Where was God to lend a helping hand?
His family and friends were al there to help him,
As he struggled to survive without his limb,

But he came through as we hoped he would
Maybe God was helping when he should
As I look at him now so confident and tall,
I hope I turn out like him after all.

Daniel Butler (15)
St Thomas More High School

SCHOOL'S HOMEWORK

Every morning it's the same,
Downstairs is mum, bawling my name.
'Wake up, you silly little fool,
Or else you'll be late for school!'

So, I run downstairs, mum's still making a fuss
'Hurry up Libby, or you'll miss the bus!'
And I run downstairs, grasping my 20p,
With my jumper tag sticking out, for all to see.

I get to school, first lesson PE (I've forgotten my kit!)
But the teacher wasn't hard on me, she told me to sit.
The lessons fly by, school is almost done,
Nearly time for all the fun!

But alas! I have homework today,
So I can no longer go out to play.
Arrgh! This homework lark, it's not fair
But I'll get it done quickly, so there!

Liberty Woodward (11)
St Thomas More High School

SCHOOL FOOL

School isn't cool
Because it makes you look like a fool
A fool in maroon,
Like a cartoon.
PE, CDT, geography, history,
All need sharp memory,
But, forget your homework
And you're history.

Alia Saidan (12)
St Thomas More High School

STATISTICS

If 70% of the world is made up of water
Why don't we live there?
If 20% of the population are naturists
Why don't they live bare?
If 75% of a day is spent working
Why don't we live more?
If 80% of crime can be stopped
Why do we have law?

How many times do we think about life?
How many times does a man think of his wife?
How, what, where, when
How, what, where, when.

If 90% of British fans support Man U.
How come everyone hates them?
If 60% of the population is women
How come we see more men?
If we spend 5% of our lives on the toilet
Why don't we eat less?
If we have a world made 2% of rubbish
Why do we avoid the mess?

If 95% of statistics are made up on the spot,
Why do we believe them?

Andrew Nesbitt (16)
St Thomas More High School

SMILE

Here's a message to the newborns
waiting to breathe.
If you believe then you can achieve
just look at me.
Let these words be the last to my
unborn seeds
Help me raise my young nation in
this world of greed
My aim is to spread more smiles
than tears
'Cause of the lessons learnt from my
childhood years.
Maybe mama had it alright as she
rests her head.
Straight conversation all night as we
bless the dead.
As they push me to the gates of
Heaven and let me picture for a while
how I lived from my days as a child
I wonder now
If God will help me live when I'm burried
Now I know deep inside only a few
love me
I leave this here and hope that
God will see my heart is pure
Is Heaven just another door?

Andrew Turnbull (15)
St Thomas More High School

COULD BUT CAN'T

I could get an A-star for my English essay but I can't be bothered to write it.
I could make my own fire but I can't be bothered to light it.
I could be top of the class but I can't be bothered to go to school.
I could be a jester but I can't be bothered to be a fool.
I could be a great footballer but I can't be bothered to train.
I could be a farmer but I can't be bothered to wait for rain.
I could play the guitar but I can't be bothered to learn it.
I could have lots of money but I can't be bothered to earn it.
I could swim the Atlantic but I can't be bothered to face the cold.
I could be a great origami artist but I can't be bothered to make the folds.
I could be nice to others but I can't be bothered to 'make the effort'.
I could be the hardest kid in school but I can't be bothered to fight.
I could lift a ton of bricks with my little finger but I can't be bothered to use my might.
I could be a DJ on Radio One but I can't be bothered to talk.
I could do the Pennine Way but I can't be bothered to walk.
People call me lazy; but I don't care
For not being lazy is too big a dare.

Andrew Hall (15)
St Thomas More High School

AT NIGHT

Frost is forming on the window pane,
Suddenly everything seems the same,
A mist falls upon certain things, not knowing,
What happens when the wind is blowing.

The icy formations glisten and shine,
I hope one day the icicles could all be mine,
But until then I must now stop,
To await the morning dew drops drop.

Snow has begun to fall,
Like a baby's first chance to crawl,
This sleepy town will wake up soon,
But there, up there, still shines, the moon.

The sky is mostly clouds of white,
But in the sky there is a light,
A star so fresh, just seen by me,
Shining as bright as the calm blue sea.

Leanne Thomasson (15)
St Thomas More High School

MUG

She's been there in bad spots.
Helped me through times,
When I thought there was no hope,
But there's always a big place in,
my heart for the mug.
But when she nags and nags
and nags
I can't stand it no more.
She is like a bad itch that won't go away
No matter what you do to get rid of it
it still won't go away.
It's constantly there, like tapping you
on your shoulder,
But when you look around,
Everything is sober.
She's been there in bad spots,
Helped me through times,
When I thought there was no hope
But there's always a big place
in my heart for the mug.

Katie Watson (16)
St Thomas More High School

BULLY ON THE BUS

I walk home from school too scared to get the bus.
Tomorrow comes but far too early.
I walked to the bus stop feeling worried.
As the bus pulled up I stepped on cautiously.
I took my seat by the driver's cab.
I turned and saw their eyes like statues glaring at me.
The oldest bully came over grabbed my bag and
emptied the contents on the floor.
The second grabbed my money
The driver saw I wasn't happy and asked what was wrong
I said those lads over there were bullying me so
at the next stop the driver banned them from the bus
so the bully on the bus was no more.

Ian Batey (12)
St Thomas More High School

WORK!

School is boring
School is dull
Work work work
That's all we do
Work when I'm young
Work when I'm middle aged
When I'm old I'm an
Old aged pensioner
Saturdays and Sundays
Is one little break
But as you know
You've still got work!

Nicholas Furno (11)
St Thomas More High School

SEE WHAT HAPPENS WHEN YOU TAKE THESE THINGS TOO SERIOUSLY?

It was a fresh Wednesday morning,
By the end, I was in mourning,
Why was he taken from me?

She started labour,
I went to work . . . and labour.
Why was he . . . stolen . . . from me?

I sat in the English lesson,
My mind never fully with . . . me,
Why was he . . . torn . . . from me?

He was soon born,
His chubby cheeks full of life,
Why was he . . . ripped . . . from me?

Even as I write . . . my mind is with him,
The man in grey took him . . . *sniff* away.
Why oh *why* . . . was he . . . burned out of my soul
Never to return except in my everlasting dreams . . .
Taken from me?

P-placed . . . in a . . . little draw . . . left . . . t-to . . . *sniffle* d-d-die,
This is ridiculous, for God's sake! It's only
A Cyber Pet!

Duncan Wild (15)
St Thomas More High School

Death Is The Point Of Life

What is the point of school?
And getting educated,
We're all going to die.

What is the point of eating?
It's a waste of time,
We're all going to die.

What is the point of Coronation Street?
We will never see the end,
We're all going to die.

What is the point of this poem?
It's not going to make a difference,
We're all going to die.

What is the point of people?
In 200 years we'll all be dead,
We're all going to die.

What is the point of *life?*
We're all going to die,
What is the point . . .
What is the point . . .
What is the point . . .

Robert Slone (15)
St Thomas More High School

GRAFFITI

Why do people graffiti?
It makes the streets look a mess,
And graffiti tells the law who's done it.
So why do people do it?

To show people they are good artists.
Graffiti is its own form of art.
They tell the follower who done it.
That's why people do it.

Why on other people's property?
Why not make their homes a mess?
People would still see it,
So why not on their own?

Other people have better walls,
To produce art on, not a mess,
Not enough people see the inside
of my house.
That's why other people's property.

Adam Jobson (15)
St Thomas More High School

SCHOOL

School is boring
School can be fun
School can be a
treat for everyone.

Having discos going
on trips
School can be fun for everyone

Steven Lee (11)
St Thomas More High School

LOVE AT SCHOOL

Love at school
Is made for fools
I mean it only lasts a week
There are no tears, it's really weird
But I know boredom has a peak
There isn't any communication
You seem to share her with the nation
In this case privacy is the word
If my friends knew this I'd have my bird
They never seem to go away
If they did it'd make my day.
Even kisses are set up, it's nothing like telly
And even then your knees turn to jelly
Now I don't even want a girlfriend
But my love life'll be on the mend
'Cos ye see I never learn
In a few weeks it'll be my turn
'Cos ye see love at school is daft
I should be in it for a laugh
Who's at fault the lass or the lad
I think the lass but I must be mad
I'll get an earful from my mate
And not to mention no more dates.
Phew!

Neil Leggett (13)
St Thomas More High School

STAR TREK: THE NEXT GENERATION

It's loved throughout the nation,
It is my favourite show!
Mr Worf's my favourite person,
He's canny big and strong,
Jean-Luc Picard - he's fair but hard,
he has to be because he's in charge!
Star Trek: The Next Generation,
I've seen every episode you're lucky,
Where did you boldly go?
You don't have to get any buses,
just step in a transporter . . .
and off you boldly go!
Star Trek: The Next Generation,
It's loved throughout the nation,
Where did you boldly go?
Where did you boldly go?
Where did you boldly go?

Ross Fletcher (13)
St Thomas More High School

FRIENDS

They will always care and look after you,
helping me out encouraging me too,
You make me laugh when I am down,
I know you will always be there
I am never sad when you are around,
through the good times and the bad
you looked out for me,
and a friend you will always be.

Elayne Chapman (12)
St Thomas More High School

MY LIFE

As we walk along the road,
hand in hand we will go.
All our love now joined together,
'N' always will be forever 'n' ever.
How much we care,
How much we've shared.
All the things we have between us.
All comes crashing down around us.
How much we care,
How much we've shared.
All those months we have shared.
Now there's no time to tell the world.
How much we care
How much we've shared.
Then the day comes we have to go,
Never to return here alone.
How much we care,
How much we've shared.
We now walk alone again.
Along that dark old road.
Until the day comes when we'll meet again.
How much we care,
How much we've shared.
Together at last, never to part,
As we walk along the road,
Hand in hand we will go,
All our love now joined together
'N' always will be forever 'n' ever.

Kate Robertson (13)
St Thomas More High School

FRIENDLY ARGUMENT

Last week I broke up with my friend,
She was telling me lies,
It was all her fault.
I started ignoring her when I found out,
That way we'd break up without a doubt.
We had a screaming match in the yard,
Bad things were said we were
finding it hard.
The next day when we came
to school,
People got involved they thought
it was cool.
Most of them said 'I'm not
taking sides,
Why not? I thought, it was her who lied!
When the bell came for the end of lunch,
We both made friends and hung
around in a bunch.
Me and my friend are inseparable.
You see,
In friendship give and take's the key.

Holly Hakin (13)
St Thomas More High School

THE UNKNOWN

It was Monday morning, first day at school.
My stomach was rumbling, my knees were shaking, I was
scared and shy.
I felt lost because I didn't know where to go.
But I was with my friends and we decided to stay together.
Later I couldn't understand why I'd been frightened at all.

Andrew Hodgson (11)
St Thomas More High School

TEACHERS

Some are fun
they are like your friends
they make you laugh.
If you do well
they are as nice as pie.
Some can be dull
like a wet grey day
if you mess up
they'll make you pay
You'll get detention
at the end of the day.
We find some lessons boring
like watching paint dry
while the teachers look forward
to the break
for some tea and cake.
Then it's back to work
like bees in a hive.

Victoria Rodriguez (11)
St Thomas More High School

HOMEWORK

Homework can be hard, as hard as genetic engineering,
Homework can be easy, as easy as pie,
Homework can be boring, as boring as watching paint dry,
Homework is the all day golf match,
Homework is the cloud which has no silver lining,
Homework is as stressful as my brother
Will someone answer
My very simple question
'Why do we have homework'?

Nicholas Jackson (11)
St Thomas More High School

SCHOOL

People running, hopping about like ants in
a nest.

People running up and down before the
lessons start.

People learning music and things, and
working as busy as bees.

People running down the stairs like
noisy traffic on the motorway.

People talking, shouting, screaming like a
shopping centre in the city.

Animals running out of school when
the bell goes at the end of school.

Christopher Hall (11)
St Thomas More High School

MY MATE

When I was asked well I was really made to
write a love poem for my mate.
I started off with hello and ended with I love
you so.
I asked him what it was for I got a simple
'I don't know'
That simple I don't know turned out to be the
one I loved since year three
The girl that had my heart but now she
has three.

Robert Chivers (13)
St Thomas More High School

HOW CAN I TELL HIM

I love him
but he doesn't know
my friends are telling me
Just to let go

My feelings are strong
I can't control
When I look at him
My eyes don't stroll

My heart goes racing
such a thudding beat
without him
my life's incomplete

The way I feel
it's hard to say
My love for him
Will last each and every day

It hurt so much
I need to tell
I really do try but
It's like being trapped in a cell

He needs to know
Just how I feel
but the feelings show
I can't conceal

How did I say
I love you so much
I don't know how
to say words of such

My feelings are deep
and it hurts so bad
when I see him with his girlfriend
It makes me so sad

I guess me and him
Just aren't meant to be
but my love will last
till eternity.

Katie Hedquist (13)
St Thomas More High School

ALL ABOUT PARENTS

Parents fight and parents fuss
although they expect the best from us
They don't mean to be bossy
and don't mean to rule
They just expect us to work hard
at school.
If you don't your life's a mess so don't
go to your parents and say you regret.
If you do remember that's your fault so
Just remember you should have worked more
hard with it.
But don't forget parents are always there
So don't feel embarrassed to go to them in a mess
Because don't forget they always care.
But when you do that's OK there's no need
to worry you won't regret because you will
know you have done something right so that
means you're getting on with your life.

Louise Adie (13)
St Thomas More High School

BULLY

Throwing names
Stones
Words
Kicking
Stealing
Grabbing
Digging
No love
Fear
Hate
I am
a
bully!

Shaun Kirkby (12)
St Thomas More High School

WHAT LIES BEYOND THE WINDOW

Beyond my window lies a
world unknown.
Words and fights that cut right to
the bone.

In the alleyways spine-chilling screams
are heard.
And people stand whimpering like an
injured little bird.

The sounds of pounding punches,
people falling to the floor.
But at least I'm safe behind
this closed wooden door.

Leanne Proud (14)
St Thomas More High School

THE FIGHT

The playground was quiet
Everyone minding their own business
Nobody arguing, nobody fighting.

Then *bang!*
People start to shout and yell.
People start running and screaming
There in the middle of the playground
Two people are fighting
Kicking and punching, shouting and screaming
Everybody is watching shouting things to
the people.
'Teacher' someone shouts
Then everyone runs from out of sight.
The playground quietens down and goes
back to being normal.

Heather Wade (13)
St Thomas More High School

FRIENDSHIP

Friendship is a very important thing
If you don't have friends you can't have anything
I've got lots of chums
so I'm not in the slums
All of my friends are really canny
'I could do with some more' says me
Auntie Annie
But friends are the best
There's no doubt about it.

James Sanders (12)
St Thomas More High School

SCHOOL

To get ahead get out of bed.
Keep your cool don't play the fool
Study maths, English and French
Try hard at football just to make
The bench.

Homework homework
What a chore.
I'm sitting at the table,
There's a knock at the door
It's one of lads wanting
Me to come out.
Is that homework done
I hear mum shout
Nearly mum I'm on
Question twenty
Well answer that one and
that will be plenty.

Anthony Stobbs (12)
St Thomas More High School

I'D FANCIED HIM FOR AGES

I'd fancied him for ages
I'd written on my books to him
But I'm just a friend to him
I would put a nail through my knee
I would run around starkers
I really go barkers
But would he notice me
No! he just thinks I'm his friend.

Sarah Brown (13)
St Thomas More High School

SCHOOL FIGHT

Fight, fight, fight the crowd roared,
Louis-v-Lee is today's big bout,
So there it is the first move . . . a punch,
Then *bang* a kick by Lee,
But a trip by Louis sends the opposition
to the floor,
Nothing for a while as Lee gets up,
A nut by Louis on the nose,
Sends Lee to the floor like a bag of
potatoes,
Teacher, teacher someone shouts,
Then the only thing you can hear is
            Get out.

Chris Stewart (13)
St Thomas More High School

FRIENDSHIPS

Friendships are never the same.
Sometimes you can trust your friends, and,
Sometimes you can't.
When you need support your friends are always there
So when your friends need support you too
should be there.
A friend is someone you can talk to.
You can go out and have fun with
A friend is someone who will cover for you when you're
in trouble.
Friendship is being friends.

Maria Mather (12)
St Thomas More High School

A WALK IN THE DARK

He walks along the city streets
all alone
looking, longing for someone to hold
alas, this girl he sees
does not know how he feels.

A lover's tiff
a lonely heart
He weeps cries tears of sadness
but she does not know
of his feelings for her.

Alas this girl
Sees no harm
She walks and wonders
until she sees her love again.

At last they're together
arm in arm
together forever
like star-crossed lovers.

Sarah Madgwick (13)
St Thomas More High School

MONDAY MORNING

On a Monday morning
You get the bus to school
You see somebody's jacket
You think it's cool!

On a Monday morning
You come in late for class
The teacher wants your excuse
'I forgot my late pass!'

On a Monday morning
You miss your break
'Cos you're in detention
because you were late

On a Monday lunchtime
The hall's the place to be
'Cos if I don't get there fast
There will be no chair for me.

Amanda Elsdon (11)
St Thomas More High School

COPING WITH SCHOOL

Monday morning
School is boring
Bye bye fun
Hello work!

> Tuesdays, maths and history
> English, French and RE
> Lots of homework we have to do
> Boring night for me and you!

All through the week
I wait in hope
Wondering whether I will cope!

> The weekend comes
> I'm full of joy
> It's fun for every girl and boy!

Joanne Harvey (12)
St Thomas More High School

A Fatal Fight

You can hear the echoing of screams.
You can hear the noises of punches.
People covered in scratches.
You can hear the blood hitting the floor.
You can hear the people shouting for more.
People covered in cuts.
You can hear the old ladies tut
You can hear the people roar.
People with tears in their eyes.
You can hear them fall to the floor.
You can hear all the lies
People dying.
You can hear the ambulance siren
You can hear the people sighing.
People dead because of a fight
People dead, can't see the light.

Rachelle Whillis (13)
St Thomas More High School

Finners

As big as a minibus
as strong as a tank
A bloodthirsty animal
travelling to where food can be found
To the depths of your imagination
with worlds above and below
Just a lonely fighter with raw power
who pushes and pounces
till he flies from the water
swiftly returning below.

Richard Anderson (12)
St Thomas More High School

FRIENDS

Friends are always around
And they'll lend you a pound,
If you forget your money.
They're kind and considerate
They know when you're down
They'll cheer you up
By taking you to town
Friends share good times
And they share bad
But afterwards you're
always glad
You had *friends!*

Christine Rooney (12)
St Thomas More High School

FRIENDSHIP

Friendships are never
What they seem.
When you don't want them to
they let off steam.
Friendships don't last long
After a while
they seem to be gone.
Some times they break
your heart.
And leave you
to fall apart.

Anna Smith (12)
St Thomas More High School

THINGS ABOUT SCHOOL

Every day rush to class
Bell goes
Push push
Running through the corridors

Rushing up to form
Everybody looks at me and says he's late again
Making excuses and conning your way out.

Rush rush
Push push
Up the stairs you go.

We get to PE
Oh, no I've forgot my kit
Balls rolling and bouncing
Teacher says pick it up
Kids saying shut up

Dinner time's got here at last
Good I'm starving.
You get to the line
Get to the back
Why sir
Because you ran
Oh no last again.

Steven Wray (11)
St Thomas More High School

HOW'S YOUR SCHOOL?

At school you learn
You read write and play
You have different teachers every day.
School is for nearly everyone.

School dinners fill you up
School dinners may make you hiccup
We have books, calculators, Bunsen burners
We use maps and computers
Make poems and stories

School may be cool
School may be great
School may not be your cup or plate.

Claire Allen (12)
St Thomas More High School

BULLYING

Everyday I worry,
So I run off in a hurry,
Down the street and round the corner,
They'll be waiting for me there.
I dash off through a bush in a,
Blazing *rush!*
Hoping they'll never find me,
Not again!
They're everywhere.
Huh! Bullies.
They just don't care.

Ben Walker (12)
St Thomas More High School

THE JOURNEY HOME

Extreme volume, to silent night,
Flashing on and off, each street light,
Burning eyes, burning feet,
No warm shelter, deserted street,
Relative time seemed never-ending,
Home to bed, strength depending,
Mind and body, numb from cold,
Stiffening body, feeling old,
Step by step, the only sound,
All alone, no one around,
I'm near the end, gone the wait,
Up the steps, to the gate,
Into the warmth, seal my fate.

Andrew Smith (18)
St Thomas More High School

SCHOOL

School 'huh' who needs it.
But sometimes school can be good
Like . . . breaktime, PE time, hanging around
With your friends. Bad things - work . . .
work . . . work. Some people like school
But not me. But the most
excellent superb thing about school
is *hometime.* But the most
Delicious thing about school is
Dinner time. *'Yum yum'.*

Shaun Whillis (11)
St Thomas More High School

A SCHOOL DAY

Children out to play
They are here all day
The bell goes

In maths
Drawing graphs
Pens writing
Pencils drawing
The bell goes

In English, reading time
Second lesson
Nearly break
The bell goes

Boys fighting girls writing
Catching up on homework
The bell goes

RE for one full hour
Moans and groans all around
Nearly dinner
The bell goes

Fourth lesson glory be it's science
Bunsen burners
Experiments
Bell goes

Fifth lesson
Art it is
Naughty boy gets detention
Bell goes
Hometime!

Amy Scullion (11)
St Thomas More High School

THE WORST WEEK IN SCHOOL

Playtime comes shouting and screaming,
It's really windy, rubbish is flying all
over the yard,
The teacher's shouting stop doing this
and stop doing that!
Next lesson comes
Everyone runs to their next lesson.
CDT then maths next,
Everyone says that maths is the best,
Tomorrow PE then RE,
Tomorrow comes it's RE, the teacher
asks for our homework so I look in
my bag but it's not there,
Everyone hands theirs in straight away,
'Don't worry Louise' the teacher says
detention at twenty past eight,
See you on Monday morning,
Next day is Saturday, get up late,
My mum won't be saying it's half
past eight you're going to be late.

Louise Pocklington
St Thomas More High School

MY CAT (RIP)

I keep thinking, why her?
Couldn't it have been another?
I wish I could turn back time,
And bring her back into my arms.

She always had a dopey look,
Her way of saying, I love you.
I wish I could see that face again,
And tell her I love you too.

I keep thinking, it's all my fault,
I shouldn't have let her out.
But her face was so pleading,
As if she knew she had to go.

I know now she's in a peaceful place,
A place she will fit right in.
All I can say to her now,
Is rest in peace, my unforgettable pet.

Zoe Connors (13)
St Thomas More High School

WE GO TO SCHOOL . . .

We go to school to learn,
We go to school to play,
We go to school to be educated,
We go to school for lunch,
We go to school to win,
We go to school for boys,
But we don't
go to school
for homework.

We like our friends,
We like our meals,
We don't like homework,
We like PE,
We hate *boring* lessons,
We like last lesson because it's
Closer to hometime
We like to go
Home.

Adele Corke (11)
St Thomas More High School

SCHOOL

School is cool
School is boring
PE and art are my favourite lessons
Geography is the most boring of them all

School dinners are the best
Chicken chips and beans
Imagine that
School dinners are the best

We have computers and maps
That's all right
Playtimes and hometimes I like the best
English is alright but Miss Filan is the best
Of them all.

School is cool
School is boring
But there's a lot of yawning.

Chloé Gannon (11)
St Thomas More High School

THE GREAT PYRAMID

Deep in geometric gloom
Do not open long-sealed tomb
The curse of evil then will fall
Not on one but surely all
Seek instead the greatest prize
That evil guards with six huge eyes
Follow where the mummy rests
In amongst the cobra's nest.

Steven Wood (14)
St Thomas More High School

BORING OLD SCHOOL

It's half past seven, time to get up
It's a rush to get ready on time,
As I run round the corner the
Bus is just coming, it seems
I just made it on time.

I get to school first lesson is maths,
Science, history then French. I've forgotten
My homework detention no doubt,
Will hometime ever come?

Playtime next if I can get out
Of the crush.
People all over just pushing me past.
Some going this way some going that,
Hometime seems impossible!

Dinner time now,
I think I'll have a sandwich.
Just two more lessons then I'll be
free for a whole weekend!

At last it's hometime it's been a
boring day and my bag is full
of books for another day!

Linzi Anderson (11)
St Thomas More High School

THINGS AT SCHOOL

The bell goes
Everybody rushes to class
Get crushed in double doors
Noisy corridors.

Get up the stairs into form
Everyone looks at me I'm late again.
Come here the teacher shouts
Why are you late?
I missed the bus

The bell goes
Rushing downstairs
Oh no double doors again

Balls all over the place
Bouncing loud
Teachers shouting pick it up
Children shouting shut up

Dinnertime's here good I'm starving
Get to the back why sir
Because you ran
Oh, no last again.

Lee Lannen (12)
St Thomas More High School

SCHOOL

When I get to school
I get a hot drink
to try and think
and also to read 'The Pink'

When breaktime comes
I go to the steps
to think what homework we
will get

When lunchtime comes
I have my lunch
but sometimes I get a punch

When hometime's there
I think of detention but I don't care
but when I get on the bus
someone always pull my hair
The next day, school starts all
over again.

Alexander McIsaac (11)
St Thomas More High School

LOVE

Being loved is really nice
But love can roll like a dice
It can land on lots of different sides
One is love and one is pride
One is hope and one is betrayal
Love can make you happy or
It can make you wail.

Ashlie Morse (14)
St Thomas More High School

THE TIDE

The tide comes in
The tide goes out
As guilded fishes swim about
In the sea, stars reflect
inspiring the intellect
While little children
Fast asleep
Dream sweetly
of the ocean deep
Of silky sands and seagull cries
of boats and schooners racing by
But soon this dream
will drift away
For morning comes
And with it
Day.

Emma O'Neill (13)
St Thomas More High School

A SMALL BUNDLE

A small bundle of life brought to me by you,
A miracle so tiny, so bright and so new.
A baby is so wonderful to love and to feed,
Just one night of sleep that's all I really need.
Late nights, early mornings,
A cry without any warnings.
The trust and safety in her eyes.
As she watches you from where she lies.
A miracle so tiny, so bright and so new,
A small bundle of life brought to me by you.

Laura Tindle (15)
St Thomas More High School

THE END

How can pain ever be beauty?
Kill those who hate us
Those who make us cynical,
Destroy our dreams.
In the shadows that shield the light,
Saving power is removed.

Crumble away those pretences,
Love who you are.
Have the strength to confront,
Retreat from the despair.
Burn all the regrets,
Watch them disappear.

Past and future combine,
An abyss of nothingness.
Awe, wonder and questions,
No true previous knowledge.
Books only full of facts,
Empathy or sympathy?

Where has childhood gone?
The memory of happy days?
No chance to live again.
History beginning now,
Searching in contentness,
Striving for acceptance.

Judith Brown (17)
St Thomas More High School

FRIDAY AT SCHOOL

Lesson ends,
All the feet begin,
With a pulled out shirt
And chewing gum in.

The feet begin, to the next class
With a big satchel
And the sound of shattered glass.

After lunch, all the children inside,
take a trip out of the door,
into a merry-go-round ride.

It's Friday, last lesson
their teachers kind,
She lets them out early
And follows behind.

Jade Coleman (11)
St Thomas More High School

BEING IN LOVE

Love takes care and kindness
With love you can have great happiness
You can overcome any great difficulties
With true love nothing matters
Love is a two way road when it comes
to hardship or joy
It can also mean getting through difficult
times together, helping your love
Being in love can bring happiness for
the rest of your life.

Mark Reay (13)
St Thomas More High School

GRANDA

You don't really think till it's too late.
Well that was my problem
Last week he came to my house
Just like normal, every night he used to come
He had been for a drink
But only two pints he used to say

He sat in the chair, his chair he would say
He started talking to me
but I was watching TV or something
I was tired and I thought to myself go home
I can't be bothered with you.

So I phoned him a taxi, and when it came
I thought thank God.
He told me he loved me and kissed me
and I did the same

That was the last time I saw my grandad
apart from when I visited his cold tired body
In the Chapel of Rest
I thought to myself please take one more breath

But now I think of it this way
God looked down and saw his tired face
and took him to rest
and I know God only takes the best

But why do I feel so empty, so much remorse
and when I think I know
It's because I never got to say goodbye.

Cheryl Robinson (15)
St Thomas More High School

MONTHS

Why do we have twelve months in a year?
Why? Tell me why?
They always seem to drag on, while
others just wander by.
The summer months are the best,
lazy, hazy, crazy days of rest.
Winter months are the worst,
Snowy, dark, cold nights.
Where do all the months go to?
Does someone take them from us?
Just when you thought they had all gone,
another twelve creep up on us.
The part I hate is the so called 'Merry
month of May', let me tell you, it's not so
merry when you're stuck in an exam hall
nearly every day for a week!
Why do the months come and go?
Forcing us to change our outfits to and fro.
Roll on birthdays, roll on Christmas, roll
on every special event, but most of all
roll on your final exams because who
knows what you might get!

Sarah Milne (14)
St Thomas More High School

WEEPING WILLOW

Weeping willow, dry your tears,
Today and tomorrow were yesterday's fears.
The joys of today are tomorrow's regrets,
But the sorrow of yesterday no one forgets.

Weeping willow stand up tall,
The birth of tomorrow will shelter us all.
Lift your branches, let stormy clouds clear,
And you, weeping willow, will shed no tear.

Christina Jackson (14)
St Thomas More High School

FANTASY

In my fantasy Boyzone would see me,
They'd bend over backwards just to meet me,
Us kids could cry,
Without having to explain why,
They'd be no fighting and all wars
would cease,
And all the world could live in peace
But it'll never happen . . .

In my fantasy people would never die,
They'd never have to live a lie,
Us kids could fly,
Up up up away in the sky,
They'd be no fighting and all wars
would cease,
And all the world could live in peace
but it'll never happen . . .

. . . As it's a fantasy not reality.

Elaine Phillips (15)
St Thomas More High School

THE X

My ex-boyfriend was a complete pain,
He gave me a headache every single day.
He used to spit when he laughed.
and to sum him up he was a selfish brat.
He bored me with his endless talk,
by the end I could of been an expert in football.
He had eyes like a snake's,
Which should of warned me he was a mistake.
But I followed my heart instead of
my head and stood by him in everything he did.
I realised one day I needed to become tough.
This whole catastrophe had gone on long enough.
His values were all wrong and he
thought he was 'lush',
To be fair I'm glad I gave him the push.
I won't look back or regret what I did,
releasing myself from the misery is the
best thing I have ever achieved!

Heather Backhouse (15)
St Thomas More High School

MY ONE-EYED CAT!

My cat has only one eye,
He lost his other in an accident,
And through that eye he spies,
Still looking very innocent.

He also has a broken jaw,
A jagged tooth sticks out his lip,
From his paw he flicks sharp claws,
And a ragged tail to the tip.

In his fur he has some tats,
He isn't very clever,
He really is a scraggy cat,
But to us he will always be as sweet as ever!

Vicki Edwards (14)
St Thomas More High School

PARENTS! KIDS!

Mum can I have these jeans?
No.
I need them desperately.
Huh.
Everyone else has them.
So.
My others are too small.
Fancy.
Stomp. Stomp. Stomp. Slam.
She thinks I'm made of money!
I hate her!
It was trainers last week!
She hates me!
I hate my life!
She could use her own money.
I could use my own money.
She can buy them herself.
I can buy them myself.
Fine!
Fine!

Katy Loerns (13)
St Thomas More High School

LOOKING UP AT THE ENDLESS ABYSS

What is it? Does it end? Who owns it?
Who knows? Just endless darkness?
Does it lead somewhere? Round in a circle?
Maybe we'll fall off the edge.

Technology is the key
The better it is the more we know.
Scientists say there are planets
Far away are we sure.

Are they strong? Are they powerful?
Are they technologically advanced?
Is there another race more powerful
Who could crush us like ants?

Or are we just a marble round
And smooth flung in a corner?
Lost under a bed?
Never to be found.

Life is a puzzle with billions of pieces
We must start from the middle and slowly work out.

David McGuinness (14)
St Thomas More High School

THE SCHOOL BELL

We were sitting in our classroom
When the school bell rang
We stumbled to the corridor
Where a fight began

There were people pushing, shoving
trying to get through
Someone got knocked over
and landed in the loo.

We finally got out to break
it had all been such a pain
and by the time we'd all got out
it was pouring down with rain.

Rachel Robson (15)
St Thomas More High School

JUST WONDERING

Have you ever wondered
why the grass is green?
- did someone need to sneeze?
and did you ever wonder
why people look like they do?
- not the same as some of you.
Have you ever wondered
why we are here from day to year.
- we don't always share.
Did you ever wonder
why people want so much?
- like everything they touch.
The world is here for all of us
and we know good from bad
don't make hurting people a must
and don't make their lives sad!

Sarah Clark (13)
St Thomas More High School

DEATH OF A DAY

The weeping willow,
Waving its wilting arms.
The warmth of spring,
The smooth heat flows on.
Blossoming buds and busy birds
Draw spring on.
Sweet smelling scents arise 'round the willow.

The quiet chirping of birds
Is harshly broken by the pattering rain.
The sky turns dark,
And the air freezes.
It is as though life itself has ceased.

Suddenly, a horrendous clash!
Thunder.
Lightning.
The beetles scurry.
Helpless birds seek refuge.
The willow droops lower.
It seems the fun is over;
A restless giant stomping closer.
When will it end?
No one knows.

Trudi Pemberton (15)
St Thomas More High School

NAIL VARNISH

So many colours
So many brands
And at so many prices!
Greens and blues and reds and pinks,
Purples and oranges too!
And there's all of those glittery ones
But!
No matter what colour
What brand
Or what price
(Or whoever buys it for you)
The same thing will happen
Even strangely at night.
And it's such a mystery
And a tragedy too
And it leaves you feeling completely confused.
You do know what I'm talking about?
I'll be worried if you don't.
'Cause it happens to everyone.
You know what I mean!
You don't do you?
Well I do!
It chips!

Felicity Parker (14)
St Thomas More High School

EMOTIONS

Feeling happy,
Feeling sad.
Feeling guilt,
Feeling glad.
Cheerfulness and depression,
Each one is an expression,
Of the way we feel inside
Of the things we cannot hide.
The way I feel I cannot deny
But the thought of him sends me sky high.
People tell me who I could have had
But loneliness can drive you mad.
It took years to make this match
All I can say is what a catch.

Laura Wellden (13)
St Thomas More High School

FLORIDA

The heat immense
The boiling sun
Red hot sands.

Glistening beaches
Soothing sea
Ice cold pools

Loud, bouncing music
Pounding rain,
And the humid evenings form

It's Florida.

Stuart Anderson (14)
St Thomas More High School

LOVING YOU ALWAYS

I wish I'd have known,
right from the start,
that as we got older,
we'd grow apart.
If I'd have known,
I'd change things of course,
then I might not feel,
so much remorse.
When we were young,
We were always together,
I took it for granted,
that we would be forever.
I moved to a different area,
not too far away,
but we saw each other less,
and less every day
but we were there for each other,
and we were still close,
and when we got together,
you couldn't separate us.
But now I try to remember the laughter and
face that I can no longer hear or see,
because you were killed by a knife,
and taken from me.

But deep down inside
you'll leave me never
'cause it's Rachael and Hal
Together forever.

Rachael Findley (15)
St Thomas More High School

LADS

Blonde hair, black hair, brown hair,
Blue eyes, green eyes, brown eyes,
Tall, short,
Old, young,
White, black,
It doesn't bother me at all

Personality is the most important,
It depends on whether they're ignorant or funny,
Stupid or canny
Or whether they really care.

Their attitudes stink when it comes to relationships.
They blank you
When their friends are around
And love you when you're alone.
They can look at other girls,
But when you look at men they call you names.
Lads always compete with each other
And think they're better than the rest,
And when it comes to relationships.

Oh sure they are the best

There's not a perfect guy, in the whole entire world
You just have to mix and match,
To find your perfect catch.

Claire Goodwin (15)
St Thomas More High School

A PERFECT LIFE

Wouldn't it be great if
you could have a perfect life,
Wouldn't it be great if
the chocolate that we ate
wouldn't put on any weight.
wouldn't it be great if
you could have the perfect date,
wouldn't it be great if
everything was free
and everything for me,
oh wouldn't it be great.

I could wear what I want
and do anything,
spend the day how I like
and learn how to sing,
I could have the clothes I've dreamt of
and the shoes to match,
I could live in a cottage
with a roof that is thatched.
This is how my life would be
if everything was up to me.
Wouldn't it be great
Oh wouldn't it be great.

Alexandra Gray (15)
St Thomas More High School

THE FUTURE

Choices, choices, everywhere.
College, six form, GNVQ
This step, that step
This course, that course.
Choices, choices, everywhere.

Decisions, decisions
Right or wrong
Whether to leave or stay on.

Pressure, pressure everywhere.
Here, there, do this
Oh no, not that.

Friends, friends, everywhere.
Leaving, staying, moving, working
Which of these will truly please

Study, study, everywhere
A, B, C, D
Nervous, study, nervous, study.
Fear, fear, everywhere.

Competition, competition, everywhere.
This job, that job, need job, want job.
Choice, choices, everywhere.

Sara Todd (15)
St Thomas More High School

THE FOGIES

The world is losing space,
Everyone gets old and never dies,
Old fogies who used to be young and beautiful,
Are now too old to play checkers,
They fought for many years in wars,
For your future,
For my future,
And how do you repay them?
How do I repay them?
With a small flat in south-west Leeds.
We are their spoilt children.
Day in, day out they do the same things,
They Hoover, read the papers and watch the telly,
Constant repetitions of the news and Australian soaps
                              become close friends,
November the nineteenth: trip to Morecambe
'Put the kettle ont' stove, George. Big day ahead.'
'Might need a Pacamack as it's cold out.'
'Shall I tek' chair? Or won't we walk far?'
'Do you need a stick?'
'Aye, an' me cap'
The bus fills up and many old women sing.
George can't hear, he's deaf.
Marion and Edith comment on their grandchildren,
George and nan don't have any.
'Pardon?'
'He cannot hear ya, he's as deaf as an auld dog'

The bus stops.
Old fogies,
'It's a shame'
really.

Paul Appleton (16)
St Thomas More High School

A DAY AT THE RACES

We got to the track,
and the queue was far back.
We got through the gate
and bought a programme.

We looked around the paddock,
then found a spot and settled down.
The cars came on the track,
for their final warm-up laps.

We got into the pit lane and got some
autographs,
You could smell the fuel and oil,
the crowd's excitement began to boil.

The cars came back on the track,
while the noise knocked you back.
The lights turned to green,
and the tyres began to scream.

The race was terrific,
but the accident was horrific,
as a car ploughed off at the
bottom of he hill.

It came to the end of the race,
with an exciting look on the driver's face
He took the trophy and sprayed the
Champagne.
And that was a day at the race track.

Paul Sharp (15)
St Thomas More High School

WAITING . . .

My granda wasn't well that day,
My auntie phoned the surgery.
The doctor said he was on his way
This was quite an emergency.

Waiting . . .
      Waiting . . .
            Waiting . . .

Two hours later, no doctor yet
I then frantically called 999
My auntie was beginning to fret
We were told by doctors 'Now he'll be fine.'

Waiting . . .
      Waiting . . .
            Waiting . . .

The nurses reappeared with a black face
'I'm sorry. There's nothing we could do'
My heart, now broke began to race
I blame the surgery, I hope you would too.

Waiting . . .
      Waiting . . .
            Waiting . . .

Mourning on the sitting room floor
And then there came that knock
My auntie, still weeping opened the door
There stood the doctor - what an angry shock.

Victoria Gallagher (15)
St Thomas More High School

GONE

I realised at the age of nine,
that I was quickly running out of time.
My friend was stolen from my life.
It was like having my heart, torn
                    apart by a knife.

It doesn't happen to someone like me,
but it does - I know - this made me see.
I sobbed all morning, all night and all day.
He hadn't done anything, but was made to pay.

It was obvious God had only lent him to us,
And now he wanted him back.
He must be in a better place,
But on Earth he's left -
A gap.

Sharon Mackay (15)
St Thomas More High School

THE FATE OF THE POET

Poems can come from anywhere
Some have a point and some don't care
Some poems are witty and some are sad
Some poems can lift you when you feel bad
But although this may make you sigh
The best move for a poet is when they *die*
A terrible fact indeed I agree
But this is the way it has to be
So watch out for poets, because it's their fate
To be acknowledged when it's too late.

Stephen Telford (14)
St Thomas More High School

I LOST MY GRANDAD

I lost my grandad on a cold winter's day
The news got to me and my heart ran away
Now I don't care if the wind blows
Now I don't care about the rain
It all does not matter ever since that mournful day
He was my guiding star my one and only
The one that helped me through
Now I don't care about the sunshine
Now I don't care about the snow
It all does not matter ever since that mournful day
He made me laugh when I was sad
And when I was sad and had a frown he would fool
around just like a clown
He kept me on the straight and narrow when I began to
stray
And he helped me through the fray
He was the best in the world
Well he was to me
But life moves on and I must too
Think of all the good times and forget the few bad
It's a big world out there
And I must devise a way to get to my destination
For I am lost without him in the vast seas of time
But I know I will get through
And see him again
All happy and gleeful
In that place we all call home
Though I miss him very much I know he is happy up
wherever he is
I just wish I could tell him I love him once more.

Steven Robinson (13)
St Thomas More High School

WHY?

Why are birds born in eggs,
Why do people grow,
Why are people grumpy when it rains,
But cheerful in the snow?

Why is a rugby ball shaped like it is
Why is a football round,
Why is the sky so high in the air,
So way above the ground?

Why do flies always fly in my eye,
Why have verbs and nouns,
Why have socks, why have shoes,
Why have cities and towns?

Why have a sun, why have a moon,
Why have birds in the sky,
Why have paper, why have pens,
Why have eggs to fry?

Why is the Earth shaped like it is,
Just like a big round ball,
Why do we live for so many years,
Why are we alive at all?

Gary Larkin (13)
St Thomas More High School

SCHOOL

School is like a very small rainforest
Where we are blossoming flowers
And teachers are fully grown trees.

Sian Quinn (11)
St Thomas More High School

BULLYING

School is good,
School is bad
Sometimes school can be a drag
Teachers are good
Bullies are bad
I don't know,
I need a hand!

My friends are there, to help me
Oh can't you see it's elementary
I try my best, oh can't you see
Why won't someone come and help me?

People say I am a swot
All I do is work very hard
I try my best, oh can't you see
Why does everyone pick on me?

Lunchtime comes
I just can't wait
For peace at last
From my dreaded fate

Another lesson begins
The teasing starts
Why am I such a bright spark?

Hometime comes
The bell is rung
Oh thank you God
Another day is done

Life like this
It should not be
School is good
It should be for me.

Craig Wilson (13)
St Thomas More High School

QUIZZED AGAIN

He rang on the bell, I ran and grabbed his hand,
We walked swiftly away, I was going to make a stand.
We arrived home late, this would be ammunition for them,
I crept upstairs, they weren't going to quiz me again.
Then out of the blue, 'Can you not tell the time?'
'Here we go' I thought, 'Dad it's only half past nine.'
'That's not the point you've got homework tonight,'
'Mum it's not a weekday it's a Saturday night.'
'Now just listen young lady, no matter what night of the week,
You'll come in on time, so just rid yourself of that cheek.'
'Dad, I'm thirteen years old, stop treating me like a kid,'
'Don't you speak like that, as from now I forbid,
You seeing that boy, he's a bad influence.'
'Dad you don't even know him, just give him a chance.'
'I don't need to know him to know that he's not right,
For our little girl, our precious little pearl.'
'Now just go to your room, change out of that dress,
It's far too short, it makes you look a mess.'
'Dad, don't start telling me what to wear,
Next it will be, 'Take off that make-up,' and, 'Take down your hair.'
'Dad, don't you understand, I'm growing up,
Soon I'll be too old to act like a pathetic little pup.'
'Dad you're really pushing me to the limit, every single day, every
single minute.'
'Dad you're ruining my life don't you understand?
To make matters worse I think you're enjoying it, I think you think
it's grand.'
'I would never do that, to make you upset or sad, even angry or mad,
Listen I'm only doing the things required for me to do as a dad.'
'Ooh! Sometimes I feel like I'm tied up by an invisible piece of rope,
With parents like you, I don't know how I cope.'

Samantha O'Toole (13)
St Thomas More High School

GANGSTERS

The gangsters down at Sunny Bay
waited outside the bank all day.
Everybody thought they had went clean
but I knew that they were real mean.
They had went down before for the same sort of job.
Not many people knew the boss was called Bob.
All of a sudden it was boom boom boom.
Their shotgun could of blown someone to the moon.
The alarm went off and the brothers came out.
Suddenly there was an enormous shout.
All of a sudden Bob went down
The others turned and gave a frown.
The brothers shouted the cops will be here
And they all ran to the car in fear
The cops were in hot pursuit
and the brothers had lost most of the loot.
They had finally gotten away
and left the region of Sunny Bay.
They thought all their troubles were over
until they saw a big black Rover.
The cops were back on their trail
and then there was a gun bullet hail.
The tyres were popped on the car.
Soon the brothers wouldn't get far.
The brothers were soon in a frenzy of smoke
They thought it was a mental joke.
They are all now back in jail.
They just don't believe they failed.

Mark Grey (13)
St Thomas More High School

UNCLE

Normal Sunday what a bore,
Off to my nana's just before 4,
10 past bus is what I got,
there before half past,
5 of course,
got to the gate and there he was,
Gave me a big welcome of 'Come in little sport,'
Grandma and granda watching TV,
their very first words,
'do you want a cup of tea?'
I sat down next to my Uncle Graham,
Totally silent in his own way,
listening to my nana rattling on,
My uncle and granda never said much,
When they did it sounded double Dutch,
Never mind I love them for what they are,
It's a shame they're not going to be here,
to see me when I'm 24.

Eddy Armstrong (13)
St Thomas More High School

NOTHING BUT FOOTBALL, FOOTBALL AND FOOTBALL

Football is the greatest game, there has ever been
lots of people like it they all follow their own team
It occupies my mind, during the day during the night and in my dreams
I always want a kick about or to go on coaching schemes

I like to go to a match and have a laugh
without any fights or hassle
But that seems really stupid and daft
Sitting in the away end supporting Newcastle

To me football is an addiction an obsession
If I could I would make it my profession
But at this time it fills me with glee
Just to see a goal scored by Rob Lee

I play in sun, snow and rain
I think Alex Ferguson is a pain
I love kicking a ball against a wall
I can think of nothing but football, football and football.

David Mooney (13)
St Thomas More High School

ANGER
(Dedicated to my brother Nicholas, whom this poem is about)

The volcano of fire that's
about to blow,
Dad's favourite china plates
I'm about to throw.
The rush of hate that's come
over me,
This maddened person I've
turned to be.
The glow of rage,
the furied scream,
I can't explain how he made
me feel.
Yes this boy just had to
look,
At my most, most secret
book.

Kathryn Smith (12)
St Thomas More High School

THE ROUTINE TO SCHOOL DINNERS!

When the bell goes at 12.20,
The parade of people is all
battered and bent!
We have to travel in an unnecessary way,
To get to the dinner hall on a particular day.
The kids go storming in like an
army at war,
but there's always a man waiting
behind the door.
(Like a policeman on patrol)
Minutes later you get to the front
of the queue and pick up your tray,
But surprise surprise it's greasy in every way,
(Especially on the 23rd of May)
You decide to order chips and gravy for lunch,
But when it comes round to
eating them, they're as 'hard as the
hobs of hell',
So you decide to give them
to Michelle.
Seven minutes later the bell goes,
And you're off to afternoon registration.
Lunchtime went so quick yesterday,
I wonder what it's like today!

Jessica Graham (11)
St Thomas More High School

MONDAY MORNING

Where has the weekend gone?
It was as quick as a cheetah.
I am a sloth, getting out of bed.
I stagger to my wardrobe and put on my uniform.
My jumper is a straight jacket,
My tie is a noose around my neck,
My bag is a ball and chain that drags me down.
In the school playground I wander around,
One of the hundreds of zombies there.
The week crawls by, as slow as a turtle,
At last, Friday night comes, a drink in the desert.
I wake up to Monday.
Where has the weekend gone?

Patrick Newman (11)
St Thomas More High School

WINTER DAYS

Frosting on the windows
Snowflakes falling down
A white icy blanket lying on the ground

Hills like tops of mountains
Children sledging down
Their cheeks turn rosy pink as they laugh and play around

People walking through fresh crisp snow
The icy wind in their face
They know where to go

Home!

Nicola Ritchie (14)
St Thomas More High School

FOOTBALL (THE MATCH)

Kick off! The referee blew his whistle
and the team who kicked off were Partick Thistle

The first shot came after 5 minutes
it is a close game but who will win it?

The fans chanted and shouted
who's going to win, Rangers! I doubt it

After 35 minutes a goal was scored
and the fans shouted 'Sack the Board'

After the break the score became level
scored by the new signing, Phil Neville

After 90, the scores were the same
we'll go into extra time in this great game

At the end, it was Rangers who won
on penalty kicks, brilliantly done!

John Nesbitt (14)
St Thomas More High School

GUINNESS

As he slides into the glass
He dresses himself with an evil black cloak
And shines on you with a touch of class
As he redeems himself with a white top hat

His sinister smile leads you on
You think about giving in
You can't resist
He's going to win!

Temptation when your throat is dry.
You open your mouth
And clear your throat
The glass is lifted
Black velvet starts to flow

You feel the sensation, cool and fresh
As you start to grow a moustache
Of white froth across your lip
Which the Guinness has left!

Daniel Thirlwell (14)
St Thomas More High School

MR WOLF

Little seal swim away,
Mr Wolf is here to stay
He's not leaving till he's full
In your flesh his teeth will pull.
Gliding around beneath the sea,
Looking for food for his tea,
Then he spots the little seal,
Yes that's it, his ideal meal.
7 o'clock not long to go,
Come along to watch the show,
8 o'clock now he's here,
Feel his presence he's so near.
9 o'clock see him glide
Little seal you better hide.
10 o'clock his hunger shows
The smell of blood drifts in his nose.
11 o'clock he sees his catch
This will be the seal's last match.
12 o'clock it's dinner time,
Little seal now you're mine.

Rachel Usher (12)
St Thomas More High School

BOREDOM

Three quarters of an hour
I've been waiting in this queue
Standing in front of a man
Who's got the 'flu.

Three quarters of an hour
I've been waiting in this queue
Wondering what the hell I could do.

What's that baby doing over there?
I know it's rude to stare . . .
But he's pulling that old lady's hair
How unfair.

Three quarters of an hour
I've been waiting in this queue
My hair has gone grey
As has my mood.

Three quarters of an hour
I've been waiting in this queue
Hooray! At last!
I'm going through!

Hannah Docx (12)
St Thomas More High School

TEACHERS

Teachers are dogs,
Their bark is worse than their bite.
They can be funny and fun,
But complain if you don't get your work right.

They work through the day,
And also the night.
They sort out our problems,
Like when we fight.

We should agree with them,
Because they are right.
But we don't,
Instead we just fight.

Heather Laing (11)
St Thomas More High School

SCHOOL!

School is a prison
They lock you up in a cell
They chain you up in
uniform and class is
really hell.
The teachers they're like
Robots they snap at
you all the time
'Pick that up'
'Put that down'
'Homework back on time'
'I am a human! Not a
Robot! I've got
feelings! Can't you tell?
So somebody come and
get me 'cause
school is really hell!'

Hold on wait a minute
Netball's starting now
Hockey, gymnastics,
Choir, football,
Wow!

Sarah Thomas (11)
St Thomas More High School

TEACHERS!

Teachers are like barking dogs,
Always going on at you.

They are as boring as watching
paint dry.

They can be nice sometimes, but
Sometimes as stubborn as a mule.

Teachers can be bossy, they tell you
What to do, they give you lots and lots
of homework.

Teachers think they're important like
A king or a queen.
If you don't do as they tell you, they
Give you a big lecture.

Some teachers are volcanoes, sitting there
Puffing and grunting at you, until they
Explode!

Some teachers are like treacle toffee all
Soft and sweet,
While others are like nut brittle,
Tough and hard to crack.

Teachers come in all shapes
And sizes, like Christmas
crackers they're full of
surprises!

Gemma Gow (11)
St Thomas More High School

HOMEWORK

The teacher enters the classroom,
His eyes as sharp as a dart,
He calmly sits behind his desk,
And then the questions start.

'Where's your homework, sonny boy?
It's time it should be in.'
'Sorry Sir, I did it but me mum
put it in the bin!'
'Then bring it in tomorrow,
I want to see it soon.'
'Sorry Sir I can't do that, I'm going to the moon.'

'Look at this you stupid girl,
It is a real mess,
It makes me really sad,'
'Sorry Sir, it was not my fault,
It was written by my dad.'

'Look at this boy,
You'd think it had been chewed,'
'Sorry Sir, it was not my fault,
My dog thought it was its food.'

'I've had enough,' the teacher yelled,
'I've heard all you've said,
I really can't take any more,
I'm going home to bed.'

Anthony Jewitt (11)
St Thomas More High School

TEACHERS

Teachers when they talk go on like broken records,
They think they are exciting us but they are
Boring us badly.
Some work makes you laugh, some work makes
You think but mostly it makes you fall asleep,
Some teachers are very angry like a very
Dangerous dragon.
They are sometimes alright then they snap
Like a hungry crocodile,
When they are telling someone off they sound
Like large barking dogs.
And when they are enjoying they jump around
And look like young children,
And very few of them are alright and have a
Good sense of humour.
When they are nice they make the lessons more
Exciting, the work is easy and good fun.
Teachers can sometimes be fashionable but some
Can be very dull.
Teachers can be very nice,
But when they see our faces they change their tune
Every time.

Cheryll Binks (12)
St Thomas More High School

STARTING SCHOOL - SCARED

So many feelings,
Loneliness, nerves and excitement,
But most of all I was scared,
Scared of being alone, because . . .

It was my first day at a brand new school,
What was I going to do?
I felt such a fool,
I didn't have a clue.

My fingers curled,
The blood rushed to my head,
My stomach churned,
My face turned all red.

Would I be with my friends,
Or was I all alone?
Would I make amends?
Oh, I just wanted to go home!

Emma Daglish (13)
St Thomas More High School

A POEM OF SADNESS

Sadness is navy blue,
It smells like gas,
It tastes of bitter lemon,
It is silent,
It's a never-ending search for happiness,
It is a dark room,
A deserted town,
A lost city,
A reflection of the grim reaper,
A blend of anger, loneliness and hope,
A clear midnight sky without stars,
A lamp with no bulb,
Or a mirror with no reflection,
It is music with no sound,
A television with no picture,
The brick wall of sadness,
Is experienced throughout the world.

Ryan Clegg (12)
St Thomas More High School

TEACHERS

Teachers are always barking on,
Just like the family dog.
Whereas pupils are intelligent,
Just like a prize hog.

Teachers are boring, just like watching a snail.
And as well as that they snap,
Just like a hungry crocodile.

Teachers are cockerels, doing the same thing each day.
'Hurry up you're late.'
'Oh dear, oh' I say.

When they tell someone off they sound like a horse,
But when they're nice, (which is not very often)
I suppose they're alright.

Louise McCormack (11)
St Thomas More High School

KILLER

As strong as an ox -
As quick as a lion pouncing on prey
She moves through the water swift as a bird
Looking for food to last the day

She spots a seal that will do for dinner
A minute later the razor sharp teeth dig in
like a knife in butter
Thrashing around, the shark wins the feeding frenzy

The shark soon swims off without a trace
into the sunset.

Sophie Campbell (12)
St Thomas More High School

MYSTERY RULES ALL

Each day her face grew paler,
Her eyes were drooping lower and lower,
The bags under them permanent
The tears in them, constant.

What can be wrong? We thought,
Why these tears? Why the faraway look when
You asked her what was wrong.

We walked past her house,
And listened.
Screams, whoops and something popping
Shouting, laughing and crying.

She came to school on Monday,
And told us she was leaving.
Where? We asked,
'A Caribbean cruise for two months,'
She replied, then she passed out.

All is clear now, those tears were tears
Of joy, those bags were side effects from late nights,
That pale colour, too much excitement.
The Caribbean cruise - a winning jackpot.
At least that's what she told us.

Sophie McDonnell (12)
St Thomas More High School

MY FIRST SCHOOL DAY

I walked into the classroom and then I cried,
Please remember Sir! I've just turned five.

The powdery chalk catching my breath
I felt as I, was choking in my hour of death.

My teacher's name was Mr White
He thought that I was very bright.

Everyone starting afresh, everyone new
Looking around, what do I see?
People glancing and staring at me.

The corridors were long and bare
A girl named Claire
Gave me an evil looking stare.

It was a big school, with
Lots of people
It was built tall
And had a steeple.

Now my first day is over
Oh I'm glad
To go back tomorrow
It won't be as bad.

That was my first school day.

Victoria Patterson (14)
St Thomas More High School

FIRST DAY AT SCHOOL

The smell of the classroom as I walked in,
Has haunted me ever since.
The racket of the strangers, running riot,
Scared me half to death.

Staring, gazing, terrifying eyes,
Of children all around.
The fixed glare of the blood-curdling teacher,
Focusing on only me.

The gloomy blackboard on the pale wall,
Towered above my head.
And the white, dusty residue of the chalk,
Lingered in the air.

The strange school seemed so big,
With its huge walls, I felt so small.
The endless lines of boys and girls,
Terrified me as I stood still.

My mother placed me in my seat,
And slowly walked away.
I told myself I would not cry,
Instead I bravely smiled.

I told them all 'School is great,'
But really I was sad.
The first lesson I ever had,
Was really how to make believe.

Rachel Haley (14)
St Thomas More High School

CHILDHOOD MEMORY

Sweating palms and throbbing head as I walked into the class,
My face glowing, turning red,
Please don't make me stay.

Everybody staring, looking, whispering,
Dusty white chalk in my throat,
Please don't make me stay.

Sitting, feeling all alone,
People pointing, talking at me,
Please don't make me stay.

The teacher looking with evil eyes,
She looked like a devil in disguise,
Please don't make me stay.

The classroom walls long and wide,
Seem to be falling on me,
Please don't make me stay.

Shaking, crying, *please* don't make me stay.

Louise Harrison (14)
St Thomas More High School

AUTUMN

Autumn makes me think of school,
The new football season, and days when it's cool.
The crackle underfoot of fallen leaves,
As they drift off trees and float over eaves.

The smell of smoke and burning wood,
The last few barbecues before the summer's gone for good.
I think of skies that are dull and grey
When the sun doesn't show for days and days.

The wind that blows the leaves around
And scatters them lifeless across the ground.
The shorter days and fading light
And the howling wind outside all night.

Hilary Farnsworth (14)
St Thomas More High School

Sharks!

The shark soars through the sea
Like a nuclear warhead
Aiming for me.

The bloodthirsty killer
His taste for blood
Is an absolute thriller.

His fin rips the sea
Like a diamond sharp
Razor through me.

His teeth like a hacksaw
He's solid as rock
He is absolute raw.

His tail like a knife through butter
To be precise Lurpak -
His roar is terrifying, he doesn't stutter

He's great, he's a shark
Not a cuddly bear -
His heart is pitch black dark.

Bryan Pattinson (12)
St Thomas More High School

DAY-DREAMING

What's for tea? I wonder tonight
Eggs? Or bacon? Both I really dislike

What music will I listen to?
Madonna? R Kelly? Or U2?

What will I wear? I ponder on
Jeans? A skirt? Oh! Which one?

What will I watch on TV?
Eastenders? The Bill? Nah, not me.

What will I dream in the night ahead?
My death? My future? Or the day I wed?

What homework will I do first?
Science? Maths? Which is worst?

Which book will I do for my review?
'Memory'? 'Dracula'? Or 'I Love You'?

Which CD will I buy at the weekend?
Oasis? The Verve? Oh! It depends.

'Lucy' the teacher's voice went boom!
As she pounded across the room.

I jumped with a start out of my dream
And looked at the teacher as she began to scream.

Looking at my empty page
Her face began to boil with rage.

Everyone turning, looking at me
Wondering what the problem could be.

I began to scribble with such fright
The empty page no longer just white.

My scrawny writing written with haste
I had no time at all to waste.

I finished my poem with delight
Still recovering from my fright!

Lucy Ronan (14)
St Thomas More High School

SCHOOL

5 to 9 the school bell rings,
Tuck your shirt in, straighten your tie
Take off those rings.
Pushing and shoving as you go to your
Form class,
Lots and lots of children you will pass.
Register has been taken, off to Maths.
As you walk there, fun and laughs,
But as you walk into the dreaded classroom,
All of a sudden, *boom!*
You turn into a quiet girl or boy,
In case you get told off by Mr Roy.
1 more lesson until it's break,
More pushing and shoving, oh for goodness sake.
Everyone's wishing for hometime to come,
Because when it does everyone will run.
Soon it comes, run for the bus,
Caroline falls over, out comes puss.
She gets up, never mind,
It could be worse, she could be blind.

Rachel Fisher (11)
St Thomas More High School

SHARK WATER

As strong as stones,
He'll eat your bones,
As solid as iron,
He pounces like a lion,
As sly as a fox,
He'll eat down to your socks,
The mouth-watering monster patrols the sea.
He sees a seal,
It'll be his meal,
He has so much strength,
And is so immense,
He has raw power,
And is built like a tower,
The fearful killer glides through the sea.

Angela Stoddart (13)
St Thomas More High School

SHARKS!

The Great White Shark,
How deftly he kills,
Not one single bit of seal he spills.
One ripple of warning,
And you're food in the morning.
His prey could be seal,
Which he doesn't need to peel!
His camouflage is grey,
So he's unseen to his prey.
He'll eat you all up (even your shoes),
So stay away because he's bad news.
He's as curious as a cat,
And as silent as an empty flat!

Nicola MacGregor (12)
St Thomas More High School

THE TERRIFYING MONSTER

The terrifying monster dives through the waves
with perfect grace,
Waiting for its next big chase.

He's spotted the seal all alone in the bay,
1, 2, 3, all the fish have swam away.

Slowly and silently the monster draws near,
The seal has seen him now and he's quivering with fear.

The seal fights back,
When he finds he's under attack,
He loses the fight,
When the shark takes a great big bite.

The terrifying monster dives through the waves
with perfect grace
Waiting for its next big chase.

Claire McAdam (12)
St Thomas More High School

DEAD SHARK

People smile so happy and proud
With a Great White Shark they have found
Hanging upside down with a screw and nail
The shark's face so blistered and pale
They cut open the thick rubber skin
They sell the teeth and the enormous fin
At the cameras they smile and grin
The people begin to frown
'Killing this beautiful creature
You've let us down.'

Jessica Nieurzyla (12)
St Thomas More High School

SCHOOL

Got on the bus for the first time ever
I thought I was rather clever
The people upstairs were very loud
The big kids talking in crowds
Finally we were there
I saw my friend his name is Joshua
Then I looked at my watch, it was nine-ish
So I decided to walk to English
In English I was feeling fine
The bell ran, yes! it's lunch time
Oh no I saw the bullies of the school
So I ran in the direction of the swimming pool
Finally they caught me
I wonder what they will do, I'll see
Then they gave me a kick
For the rest of the day I was off, sick.

Adam Mooney (11)
St Thomas More High School

SCHOOL

School is where you meet new friends,
School is where you come to an end,
School is where you come by law,
School is where you learn even more,
School is full of hard work,
School is where you have to look,
But beware not to act like a mule,
Or they will write that as another
                              Rule!

Avita Sharma (11)
St Thomas More High School

THE SHARK!

Mr Wolf, coming, thrushing, pushing,
through the open ocean,
1000s of pounds, below the surface,
frightening, scary, to all that might see him,

Spotted seal in the water,
Teeth are ready to make the kill
I hope the seal gets away before he will

Splashes of thunder,
Power and might,
His jaws will come down, and give you a fright,

Shark swims strong, to catch his prey,
But the seal knows he will live today.

Louise Wafer (12)
St Thomas More High School

SHARK ATTACK

From the gloom and doom
Of the ocean floor
He shoots around
Like a lion ready to roar, it turns, flips and dips
Like an acrobat performing and all the fish swiftly swim to hide
From the danger of his power, the *shark* comes and goes like a bolt
Of lightning and attacks
Like a clap of thunder
The *shark* has left now
It is calm again and drops of rain can be heard
Once again . . .

Suzanne Middlemiss (13)
St Thomas More High School

MY SCHOOL

In my school it's full of noise, and yelling, banging sounds.
It's hardly noisy in my class,
But it is in the school playground.
The bell rings and the corridor fills
With pupils, teachers too!
And trying to get to your next class,
Squashed in the middle is you!
In an hour the bell will ring again,
And who'll get squashed?
      Me!
Then the corridor fills, and everyone rushes
To the year seven assembly.
There are lots of subjects in my school you see,
English, art, plus technology.
I wonder if you have a school like mine?
To go to my school, you must be out of your mind!

Lindsay Roberts (11)
St Thomas More High School

SCHOOL

Brrrr, rings the bell
Here's the start of a living hell

I rush along the corridor and up the stairs
Taking no notice of the looks and the glares

The teachers give me detention
The headmaster threatens suspension.

Because I just long for the hometime bell
To end my day of living hell.

Kathryn Montgomery (11)
St Thomas More High School

School Time

We start off so happy and jolly,
Then the large bell rings and everyone starts to worry,
We run along as fast as we can,
Some fall like horses.

The first lesson comes and we start to boo,
But we start to cheer because I.T. is the lesson,
But that's soon over and the next lesson is geography and I
Hate it because he calls me 'Harry Old Bean',
I count the times he does it, eventually comes to sixty,
It is now break at lunchtime, I am wishing to go home.

English and basketball lessons are next,
English flies by,
Basketball bounces by,
It's now time to go home and the cheers and jeers are heard.

Andrew Harrison (11)
St Thomas More High School

School

In and out of corridor corners
Round the back of first kiss huts
Slop of that you call dinners
Everybody screaming about everything or anything
Friends are for life not Christmas
A shout there and everywhere
Teachers coming out of walls and doors
Taking those things that you just must not have.

Paula Kerr (11)
St Thomas More High School

SCHOOL

Pens and pencils out of bag
The teacher's shouting
What a hag

Next bell rings and we all pack up
We're squeezing through the corridor
People getting stuck.

Run to the hall, grab a seat anywhere
People eating packed lunch
People pulling hair.

Lunch time ends form class full
Hand in homework
And teacher? 'Raging bull'!

Last bell rings, kids flee for the door
We're free from school for two whole days
For school is a *bore*.

Alex Slone (11)
St Thomas More High School

SHARK POEM

He swims around with his flexible fin
eating and eating everything.
His jaw is big, his teeth are sharp he could
eat a metal bar.
He hits the seals with such a blow
he looks just like a torpedo
The death in the sea is very quiet
seals and fish make his diet!

Tom Johnson & Colin Davidson (12)
St Thomas More High School

MY FRIEND SMASHED A WINDOW

Football in the playground
there was me and my friends,
we ran across the playground as
fast as we could.
My friends smashed a window like
nobody should.
Over the bar flew the ball
over the fence and over the wall.
'It's swerving left, it's swerving right'
it hit the glass with quite a fright.
'Paul, you spoon'
'It wasn't me, it rebounded off the keeper's knee'
'Aim for the goal not over the wall,
Paul, you'd better buy me a new ball.'

Michael Burke (11)
St Thomas More High School

MY CAT FLUFFY

My cat Fluffy she is fat and 'Fluffy'
She plods upstairs and goes to sleep.
For nine hours she snorts and snores
Twitching and itching and dreaming about rats.
She wakes up and plods downstairs
And eats her food and goes outside
Up the fields to catch a mouse or bird.
She comes back and plays around
And after a hard day she plods back upstairs
And goes to sleep and dreams about rats.

Adam Geraghty (13)
St Thomas More High School

Is School Fun?

The people in the playground shouting
The smell of school dinners wafting out of the hall.
The sound of the bell telling us to go to lessons, it's deafening.
The wind rustling crisp packets around our school.

Going to registration where our name is called
The bell rings, who will be crushed or thrown down
The stairs by 11th year bullies?
Get out our books and start work.
If you forget your homework you'll be chopped,
Detention, extinct, what else will you get?

School is a place of execution,
Where the teachers are the executioners
And we are the victims
It is a place of *torture!*

Trying to remember: books, pens, pencils,
Who your friends are and aren't.
If you know what it's like, you'll be okay,
If not . . . now you know what's coming your way.

Kate Flanagan (11)
St Thomas More High School

A Family Feud

Swords clash, angry words fly,
I'm caught in the middle, just want to cry.
My aunts and uncles hate me, so they don't talk,
My cousins think it's all a joke.

My mother and father don't want to know,
They never let their true feelings show.
They're too busy fighting to notice me,
I might as well walk out and leave my key.

I feel all alone and on my own,
Nobody to talk to, they all think I moan.
I want to get away, far from here
Where nobody fights, or lives in fear.

Jennifer Cunningham (13)
St Thomas More High School

SCHOOL

I get on the bus with all my friends
Dreading the place where it ends

I go down a road it splashes in mud
And in the distance there it stood

As I fell over, feeling a fool
I looked up and saw a terrifying thing, school

I walk in the gates dreading the day
And then the bell goes straight away

I enter the form room, havoc in the air
Then I see Adam pulling someone's hair

As the bell goes for the second time
Oh how I hate school time

We're in our first lesson and our first class
How I'm hoping for this day to pass

But I'll get through 'cos I got a friend
And this is the last of my poem, the end.

Stephen McLaughlin (11)
St Thomas More High School

THESE I HAVE LOVED

These I have loved
The swooping, speeding flight of a swift,
The rushing roar of a jet plane tearing through the sky,
The sweet smell of freshly cut grass,
An over powering odour of burnt aviation fuel,
Flames feeding on helpless hunks of wood,
And the meandering mist which rises from a wet
forest on a cold and still morning.
The sharp shearing lines of a snow-covered mountain,
The smooth absolute beauty of Alicia Silverstone,
The unique music of a well-played guitar,
The haunted howl of a lost and lonely wolf,
The deep, dark blue of the sky after sunset,
And awesome orange emitted from an expensive explosion.
A mysterious and magnificent castle,
A dark and dangerous broadsword,
The creamy, comforting taste of apple baby food,
These I have loved.

Paul Rumney (16)
St Thomas More High School

THE SHARK

He glides across the water like a skater on ice
His teeth are as strong as steel
This dangerous beast searches the seas
To use his razor sharp teeth on elephant seals
The bloodthirsty predator eyes up his prey
He thrashes the sea as he kills the seal
Then pounce, bang, swallow, he has his main meal.

Daniel Sherliker & Karl Watson (12)
St Thomas More High School

School

School:- Creaking doors, footsteps, teachers shouting,
Blackboards squeaking, toilets flushing, people talking,
chalk scraping!

Teachers running, children getting wrong. Everybody wearing
the same clothes, everybody is identical! Boys and girls
everybody, like a child zoo!

Clocks ticking, pencils working, brains ticking. Caretakers
cleaning, dinner ladies cooking, chairs squeaking, lights
beaming, scissors chopping, money clashing, telephones, balls
bouncing!

Everything going!

Charlotte Campey (11)
St Thomas More High School

The Ups And Downs Of School

School is a massive place,
If you're naughty you can get detention or even suspension
Teachers, dinner ladies, pupils too
Oh what do you have to do
To get some peace and quiet?
Lessons, yes 5 every day, English, French, maths, art, CDT and
Home economics, I could go on forever.
But you should never ever kick people in
Or put them in bins
Or take the mick
Or punch people and make them sick
And at the end of the day I wonder will the big-uns put
Me 6 foot under.

Richard Huggan (11)
St Thomas More High School

SHARK'S DINNER

Majestic monster,
Gliding beast,
Swimming through the sea,
I've only just had dinner
But I've already found my tea.

A lonely little seal,
Separated from his pack
Will be an easy target
And an easy catch

After the fight
The shark swims off
Never to be seen again . . .
Until dawn the next day
When he pounces again.

Maria Lovell (12)
St Thomas More High School

FEELING ILL

Today I feel ill
Because yesterday I fell down a hill
I went to pick a flower
Instead I had a shower
The doctor came this morning
When the rain was pouring
I hope I'll be better tomorrow
I'm already full of sorrow
Now it's tomorrow, I'm better once more
But now my knee is sore.

Andrea Devlin (12)
St Thomas More High School

RUGBY

I play rugby 'cos it's dangerous
I know a man called Tegs.
He was running down the pitch one day
And tripped and broke his legs.

We took him to the hospital
To get his legs x-rayed,
We sat in the flipping waiting room
All the ruddy day.

Tegs went back to the pitch and
He trained hard for a match,
His players kicked the ball high
Tegs went for the catch.

All went well, he landed safe,
His legs they did him proud,
He looked forward to the away-day match,
In front of Big Boys crowd.

Broken arms and ankles
Incarcerated legs
The only person fit to play was
No *O.O Tegs!*

He is running down the pitch now
He has just past four or five,
They will pound him like a tension ball
He'll be lucky to be alive.

Tegs is running faster now
The crowd shouts loud, and roars
Tegs passes the Centre Back and . . .
Silence . . . Tegs scores.
And only the silence roars.

Peter Brown (13)
St Thomas More High School

SCHOOL DAZE

What's the time, it's half past six,
Oh no, school.
Out of bed and into clothes
The morning, rule
Later on, at ten past eight,
Catch the six eight oh,
Reach the school, 8.45,
Let out a moan,
Registration in lab three,
History,
Get out pens and pencils too,
Miss, I can't see,
What's next? Oh it's English,
With Miss Filan,
We have to write a school poem
(By the way she plays a violin)
Books, books, and more books,
I'm sick of school
Classrooms, work, and Michael Burke,
Not to mention rules,
Never mind, it's nearly time
To go,
There goes the bell!
Catch the six eight oh.

Sean Scott (11)
St Thomas More High School

THE SEASONED FIGHT

It's the fight of the year, my favourite one,
Will winter win?
Will his icy reign come?
So freezing cold and grim.

Or will our champion spring
Make winter's bell ring?
Here come the contestants. Let's begin
Here's the first round! Ring-a-ding-ding!

Spring's pretty sleepy, lying on the ground,
Winter's very fit and jumping around.
Spring's staggering up, clutching her head
Winter throws a punch
Spring's skipping away, laughing
Do I hear some birds sing?

Oh, and winter's down with a knock to the head,
A mean left hook, spring's eyes are red,
She's getting into this,
Oh look at that lamb frisk!
Has spring won?

Well let's review the facts,
Winter is melting
Spring is running riot
And it seems again
That spring is here
So let's all give a mighty big cheer!

Cliodhna Duncan (13)
St Thomas More High School

MAD

My Mam is mad she loves my Dad.
My Mam is mad she snogs him bad.
My Mam is mad she hits me hard,
My Mam is mad but sometimes sad.
My Mam is bad but mostly mad,
My Mam is crazy, but not lazy.
My Mam is nice I love her crazy.

My Dad is nice but very sly.
My Dad is quiet but on a diet.
My Dad is kind but hard to find.
My Dad is clean but very lean.
When my dad is drunk he eats lots of junk,
My Dad is lovely but always hungry
My Dad is crazy but very lazy.

Steven Brown (12)
St Thomas More High School

FIREWORKS

F ireworks, fireworks in the sky.
I really like to see them up high
R ain or snow I'll be there till the
E nd of the display,
W ould you like to come too?
O h yes I would said Aunty Lou
R ain or storm I'll be there, so will
K atherine with her teddy bear
S o, fireworks, fireworks in the sky, I love watching, up they fly.

Danielle Gibbs (12)
St Thomas More High School

FRIENDSHIP

Friendly
Respectful
Intelligent
Excellent
Novelty
Dreamy
Super
Happy
Important
Polite.

If I were being picked on,
I would scream,
'Cos I would think, it was
all a bad dream,
Why do people pick on others?
It must be because
They haven't got any sisters or brothers.

Katie Smith (12)
St Thomas More High School

BULLYING

Some people get angry
and bully other people.
They can't express their
anger any other way.
They're rough, they're tough,
they're really evil.
They're really cowards, just trying
to be hard,
But they don't impress anyone.

Andrea Follin (12)
St Thomas More High School

BULLYING

Just like a lot of things
bullying isn't fair,
The person who is doing it is
out to scare,
They're lonely, cold and sad,
They try to be really bad,
They're all alone,
In their own little zone,
They think they're the
hardest in their town,
But they're making the
victim really down,
Someone else will come along,
Big and strong,
They will lose their fuse,
The bully will lose.

Gemma Patterson (12)
St Thomas More High School

THE BULLIES

I am a victim when I go outside
When I see them I try to hide
But they always find me.

I feel very sad and low
When they hit me I feel very sore
Cause it hurts badly.

When I come home from school
I long to go safely to the pool
My Mam is very worried about me.

Shelley Butters (12)
St Thomas More High School

BULLIES

Bullies, bullies everywhere
Bullies, bullies in my hair
       If I'm there
       There there

Bullies, bullies everywhere
Bullies, bullies in my hair
       First my hand
       Then my head

Bullies, bullies nowhere,
Bullies, bullies not in my hair
       Not my head
       And not my hand
Now they're gone, and now I'm
       Free.

Alex Scott (12)
St Thomas More High School

THE BULLY

I walk to school, he watches me
I eat my dinner, he watches me
I play with my football, he watches me
I walk home, he watches me
I walk to school, he kicks me
I eat my dinner, he pours water on it
I play with my football, he kicks it away
I walk home he kicks me and hits me
He pulls my tie 'Why?' I cry.

Thomas Grist (12)
St Thomas More High School

BULLYING

Bullies can be very mean,
They are often heard,
But remain unseen.

Bullies shout, kick and punch,
And hang around,
In a great big bunch.

Bullies can be very big,
If you're small enough,
They'll give you a dig.

Bullies have no real friends,
Stick with your mates,
And you'll be on the mend.

Bullies always want
Their own way,
So take my advice,
Stay well away.

Nicola Robertson (12)
St Thomas More High School

HOBBIES

Dancing is all I live for,
It's my favourite thing,
I also like to sing and act,
Upon the stage, what a great impact

I also like to shop,
I'll do it until I drop,
I like to laze around a lot,
Especially in my pyjamas.

Jerri Fletcher (12)
St Thomas More High School

THE BULLY

A bully is evil,
A bully has no guts.
A bully gets other people
to do his dirty work.
A bully denies hitting
younger people.
A bully thinks he's really great
but when the victim reacts
the bully gets scared and runs away.
A bully does not like getting bullied
even though he's a bully himself
A bully goes around in a gang
and if they get into trouble
he blames the other people in the gang.

Stephen Connolly (12)
St Thomas More High School

WHAT A BULLY IS . . .

B ig
U gly
L urking
L ying
Y ellow bellied
I gnorant
N oisy
G reedy.

Craig Findley (12)
St Thomas More High School

WINTER GROWTH

The summer is here,
Let's give a big cheer,
It's time to put on little tops,
But when you do, one button pops.
Followed by two more.
You gasp and stare down at the floor.
All around you buttons shaped like balls.
You give a sigh and another falls.
All are gone, the boy you like stops to stare.
You feel that you're completely bare,
You pick them up, you start to run,
You trip up,
Oh what fun.
People start to laugh at you,
This couldn't be happening,
This couldn't be true,
You finally get home, oh what a relief.
With one almighty heave,
The top comes off, on with another one,
You walk out the door,
Everything's dead and gone.

Jenna Kirkwood (12)
St Thomas More High School

PUPPIES

They jump and skip and run around.
Chewing your slippers and digging in the ground.
Some with tails, some none at all.
They eat and sleep and grow so fast.
Puppies, puppies it's a shame they don't last.

Simon Boyle (11)
St Thomas More High School

MY WEEKEND SURPRISES

On Friday morning,
When I got up,
In my bed,
There was a pup.
It licked my face,
And picked my brace,
Fell off the bed,
Then it was dead.

On Saturday I found a cat,
Sleeping in my favourite hat,
It ripped my top,
And spilled my pop,
It drank Dad's stout,
So he threw it out.

On Sunday I found a little skink,
Swimming in the kitchen sink,
I put it in my pocket,
Had his photo in my locket,
I took it to my Granny's house,
And she fed it to her mouse.

Louise O'Brien (12)
St Thomas More High School

MY PET NIBBLES

I named my pet Nibbles
He nibbles here and there.
His ears are really floppy
And he has snow white hair.

He hops and hops till he drops
And he loves to drink milk
Yes he is a rabbit
And his fur is soft as silk.

His eyes are blue as the sky
I love to see him play
His age is only two
I'll cry if he does not stay.

I opened the hutch
And out he popped
Energetic and lively
With a skip and a chop.

He stays in my room
His friend is named Jibbles
His hutch is quite big
That's my Nibbles.

Steven Brierley (12)
St Thomas More High School

IF I WASN'T ME

If I wasn't me I'd be a bee,
I'd hunt for honey,
Then take it back to my queen.

If I wasn't me I'd be a pea,
Rolling round on someone's plate,
They'd try to prong me with a fork,
But I'd hide under some pork.

If I wasn't me I'd be the queen,
Sitting upright on my throne,
I wouldn't have a king, I'd sit on my own.

If I wasn't me I'd be the sea,
Sending waves high in the sky,
They'd crash back down, making an
almighty splash,
And wetting everyone in sight.

If I wasn't me . . .

Michael Barrass (12)
Southmoor Secondary School

MY SISTER

M any sisters are horrible and exotic
E ven mine was found in an astronaut's pocket
M y sister is very active at night
O n Sunday is the only time she sees light
R idiculous ice sculptures on her skull
I   n her nose there is a ring like a bull
E mma is this alien's name
S he drives everybody in the house insane.

James Knox (12)
Southmoor Secondary School

LIFE!

Tiny, wrinkled, pink people,
Crying, selfish, noisy people

Dirty nappies, dummies thrown,
Teddy bears and prams

Young, bald, bouncing people,
Happy, sad, changing people

Gaining memory, skipping ropes,
Facing life ahead

Middle-aged, clever people,
Working hard, busy people

Cooking, cleaning, housework done,
Where's the time to rest?

Active, sporty, healthy people,
Eating, drinking, social people

Extending memory, driving cars,
Now we're half way through.

Weak, kind, helpless people,
Lonely, wrinkly, lifeless people

Hearing aids, information passed,
Illness and disease

Unhappy, empty, ugly people,
Bored, deaf, exciting people

Losing memory, walking frame,
Facing death, *Gone!*

Ruth Peacock (12)
Southmoor Secondary School

NIGHTMARE

In the shadows lurks a figure, who is so grim
that he could scare a spectre out of his wits!

Weird death, (I mean, how nasty can you
get?) wears black robes and carries a
scythe with which he chooses who will be
next!

Their sidekick, Satan, is the most frightening of
the ghostly trio for he keeps a rabies infected
bloodhound!

Don't forget the bloodhounds from Hell; Rex,
Claw and Sabre are the most evil and vicious
in the pack!

The Psycho, who committed the chainsaw
massacre, is now joining forces with the
powers of evil to launch yet another gut-
flying attack!

It, the clown, is a most terrible beast who
has nails longer than lions and teeth sharper
than a razor blade!

The Black Beasties that live under your bed,
knife like claws and eyes glowing red!

Who is the creature living under your stairs,
snake like fingers and spiders in his hair!

This is Hallowe'en, this is Hallowe'en

It's All Hallows Eve!

Will you ever sleep again?

Alan Bates (12)
Southmoor Secondary School

WINTRY MEMORIES

I remember waking up to the white blanket of snow,
Covering the garden,
It reminded me of Christmas.
It was icy cold.
Snow was falling thick and fast,
It was five inches deep!

I remember the sudden heavy storm,
The humongous snowflakes,
The snow was falling in a blizzard,
The deepest it had been for years.
We ended up in a shop,
Until we warmed up.

I remember, it was so beautiful,
The garden looked so calm,
I longed to play outside.
Everything seemed to sparkle and glitter,
It was all so bright and clean,
Like something from a fairy tale.

I remember the still flakes falling,
Just right to build a snowman,
We went to the local park,
Me and my dad made a snowman,
Which we admired for days.
Later that afternoon we had a snowball fight.

I remember all my friends came round,
We went sledging,
Down the hills over and over again,
It was a few days before Christmas.
My nan came to see us
It was a day to remember.

I remember it was very cold,
It was the first white Christmas,
My dad got me a new puppy,
I could only see her tail and her nose!
My nan bought me a Mickey Mouse teddy,
I was totally surprised!

I remember . . .

Gemma Bargh, Victoria Burn (13), Janis Douglas & Phillip Gale (12)
Southmoor Secondary School

CHILDHOOD MEMORIES

My first memory was when I went to London when I was six.

Each time Newcastle loses I feel mad.

My happiest time was when Newcastle beat Man U 5-0.

Or the time when they beat Barcelona 3-2.

Riding the car with my dad and nearly crashing into the gate
every time I did it.

I remember my first day at secondary school and having all
those new subjects.

Each Christmas morning when I used to get up really early
and run through my parents' bedroom and show them the
presents that Santa gave me.

Some of my best memories are just playing games with my
brother at home.

Christopher Scott & Liam Andrews (12)
Southmoor Secondary School

THE STORM

The wind howls through the streets,
Like a wolf hunting its prey.
As the rain falls from the sky,
Like a baby crying, big, fast, drops.

The lightning flashes in the dark sky,
Like a lighthouse sending signals out to the sea.
While the thunder crashes in the sky up above
Like the waves crashing on the rocks on a windy day.

And I snuggle up in my warm cosy bed,
With a cup of hot chocolate.
As I listen to the storm outside my window,
All cosy in bed just listening,
                listening,
                       to the storm in the night.

Kay Athey (12)
Southmoor Secondary School

MEMORIES

M y best memory was when Newcastle beat Barcelona 3-2,
E ven better than Florida too.
M y third best memory was when Newcastle beat Man U 5-0,
O r that time mam bought a car from Mill.
R over is the name of this brilliant, rare car, *(Not)*
I, thought, like it a lot.
E very day she drives it a great deal,
S he doesn't know this, it has a punctured wheel.

Nicholas Lynch (13)
Southmoor Secondary School

MY SECRET PLACE

I remember my secret place,
No one knew about it except me,
It was my second home,
Behind some bushes I played there all the time.
I remember my secret place,
It was a cupboard under the stairs,
There were loads of bags so it was comfortable.

I remember my secret garden on the disused railway lines,
Covered with weeds behind a load of bushes and brambles,
There was a tiny hole in the wall,
I could sneak through it.
I remember my secret place,
It was a cupboard in my room,
I went there when I was fed up.

I remember my secret place,
At the bottom of my garden,
It was a cave made out of trees.
I remember my secret place,
It was at the back of my wardrobe,
I took a torch and no one ever found me.

I remember my secret place in my nana's back garden,
Behind a small wall,
I used to sit there to keep warm.
I remember a cupboard at my nana's house,
There was a window,
If I shut the door I would get locked in.

I remember hiding under my Grandmother's table,
No one could see me down there.
I remember the roofspace where I hid my violin,
Daylight showed where the slates were broken.

Sarah Gibson, Natalie Newton, Katherine Ramsey & Michael Barrass
Southmoor Secondary School

A TOOL

I remember a particular tool, it was a very heavy hammer. It had an old wooden handle.

I remember the garden fork, it was an old-fashioned lady's fork. Its prongs had got bent.

I remember my grandad's hammer. I thought it was wonderful, shiny on the end. Hearing that loud sound it made was great.

I remember an axe. We used it for chopping wood for our fire.

I remember a plastic hammer which I had when I was young. It was red and blue.

I remember the whirring noise of the hedge-cutter. It made a piercing and grinding sound.

I remember my dad's hammer. It was grey and had a wooden handle.

I remember my dad's monkey wrench. He said 'You can always count on an old chimp.'

I remember a hammer, when I tried to hammer a nail into a piece of wood I used to hit my thumb.

I remember a tool, at my nana's house. It was a screwdriver with lots of different heads.

I remember . . .

Laura Welch (13)
Southmoor Secondary School

THE HAUNTED HOUSE

In the misty dead of night,
beware of the devil's evil light.
Do not try to scream or run away,
they will catch up with you some day.
They'll play with thoughts inside the head,
they will not stop until you're dead.
And you will go on haunting too,
you'll join their strange but evil crew.
Never cross the haunting path,
not even for a joke or laugh.
If you do,
            they'll be after you.
So stay afar the haunted house.

Claire Lynn (13)
Southmoor Secondary School

AUTUMN

Twisting and twirling the leaves fall to the ground.
Making the place look dull all around.
Brownish reddish crinkling leaves.
Covering the floor with autumn dreams.
Autumn is my favourite season.
makes me feel like just dreaming.
All through the shortening autumn days.
The sky is filled with golden rays
And now when the autumn is over,
I wait for it to return,
With its golden leaves and pleasant dreams.

Leanne Milne (12)
Southmoor Secondary School

STAR TREK

Captain Kirk gives an order
Time for a new heading
Klingons have come over their border
Time to go, Captain Kirk is leading

Soon the Klingons come in sight
The crew are ready with phasers
Captain Kirk is prepared to fight
The Klingons' deadly lasers

Shields down to 40 per cent
yells out Engineer Scott
Then the Klingons' shot did repeat
Five phasers not Scott
Enterprise Phaser strive home
Destroying a Klingon ship
When suddenly their shields were gone
Kirk said 'Let's go, quick'
Another blast rocked the ship
Knocking the engines out
The Klingon ships then let rip
And Captain Kirk started to shout

Klingons in the transporter room
Captain Kirk gets really mad
The door explodes with a boom
Then Captain Kirk is really bad

He sets off the self-destruct
And beams down to the nearest planet
The Klingons die in the self-destruct
While the crew lie on the granite.

Soon another ship gets made
Finer than any seen before
A dangerous game Kirk has played
And now it's his turn once more.

George Quinn (14)
Southmoor Secondary School

THE ASSASSIN

The tall, cold man walked by
Wearing a black hat pulled over his eye.
He got out a knife
To take someone's life,
As he hid from the passers-by.

He glanced at his watch to check the time.
He was doing the kill at exactly nine.
He clenched his fist
As he walked into the mist.
Just then he heard the church clock chime.

He crept up the street with a heavy heartbeat.
The victim was late,
It was nine o'eight.
All of a sudden the target did appear.
He pulled out his knife, his plan was clear.

He grabbed the man and thrust in his knife.
Slowly the man loses his life.
The job is done,
The assassin is away
Until he is needed another day.

Sean Croft (12)
Southmoor Secondary School

I'M ONLY 12 YEARS OLD!

I'm only 12 years old,
I don't know very much,
I'm learning all the time,
But I need my space,
To play my CDs and cassettes,
After all, I'm only 12 years old.

I'm only 12 years old
I clean my room,
And tidy my books,
I pick up my clothes to put in the wash,
I have to do as I'm told,
Because, I'm only 12 years old.

One day I'll not need to be told,
Because I'm getting old,
When you're old you don't get told,
But for now, I'm only 12 years old.

Iain Dodsworth (12)
Southmoor Secondary School

TRAIN DISASTER

Waiting, waiting for the train to come round.
Bouncing, bouncing up and down
Hear the squeaking through the tracks,
Waiting, waiting with an aching back,
Old people step on the train,
Then suddenly, it starts to rain,
Everyone scrambles for a seat,
Then I get something to eat
The train comes to a halt
The driver shouts 'We have a fault.'

Gary Graham (13)
Southmoor Secondary School

THE RACE

The cars go swerving round the track
With some cars bashing back to back
The tyres are screeching very loud
With screams and shouts from the massive crowd.
It's a big question who's going to win
Says the commentator as the race begins.
A few laps later, time for a pit-stop
But wait, the car explodes with a very loud pop!
Must have been the engine, oh no, take a look!
A driver emerges, engulfed in flames
That poor man, he'll never be the same end of the race now,
The chequered flag waves,
A red car zooms past, he's won the race!

Emma Butler (12)
Southmoor Secondary School

MY LITTLE SISTER

My little sister is sentenced to doom,
Every time she creeps and snoops about my room.
I open my bedroom door,
And find her raking in my drawers.
To stop her being allowed in my room
There should be laws.

I pick her up and swing her round,
And toss her on my bed.
By the time I've finished with my sister,
She surely will be *dead!*

Lisa Nelson (12)
Southmoor Secondary School

B'BALL GAME

Payton has the ball and he plays it to the left,
It's nearly intercepted but it comes through to Kemp,
He does a bit of dodging then he goes for the hoop,
The Bulls ain't scored but the Sonics have two!
The end of quarter one and the teams are tied,
The Sonics and the Bulls both have twenty-five.
Into quarter two,
Jordan scores a hoop,
The Bulls are up by two,
Then the Sonics make a good move,
Perkins is involved, Payton is too,
He plays an overhead pass, then Kemp scores a hoop.
At half-time Sonics have the lead,
Bulls have fifty, but Sonics fifty-three.
Quarter three,
Bulls turn mean,
Hit a hot streak,
And are ahead by fifteen,
Detlef Schrempf is playing worst of all,
After all, he hasn't even scored!
Pippen misses a screamer,
No one can believe it,
Jordan tries to retrieve it . . .
Schrempf assists Kemp,
Then scores one himself,
Sonics catch up,
Just as time's up.
In the last quarter, time's running out,
Bulls have no time to pass it about,
So Longley decides to give it one last fling,
And to his surprise he earns them the win,
The crowd's full of cheer,
At the United Centre.

Darren Reid (13)
Southmoor Secondary School

WATER

Water is clear
Water is lame
It ripples and tipples and goes down the drain.

Water and ink
Water to drink
Water is definitely, definitely not pink.

Water is rough
Water is calm
Water for pigs to drink on the farm.

Water is dirty
Water is clean
Water trickles quickly down a stream.

Water is fast
Water is slow
Water helps the green grass grow.

Stuart Ferguson (12)
Southmoor Secondary School

NIGHT

Night is the end of dawning
Night is the darkness
Falling
Night is so very bright
Night is so very bright
Night is so bright by the beautiful moonlight
The stars twinkling up in the sky
I wish it will never ever die.

Branwen Ellison (12)
Southmoor Secondary School

Igor!

Darkness crept upon Castle Dracula
Which was right in the heart of Transylvania,
It was the home town of every vampire alive,
Once caught under their spell there is no chance to survive.

We are the victims, they are the assailant.
Human beings are what vampires hunt,
They will suck your blood until you turn pale white,
Believe me it's not a pretty sight.

Darkness arrived, Igor rose from his grave.
No one's life would Igor save,
No one's life except his own
Igor gave out a vicious groan.

Igor very slowly awoke,
You could tell he wasn't a friendly bloke.
His evil eyes and devilish smile,
Was sure to make you run a mile.

A vampire so repulsive and pale,
Is bound to look as dead as a door nail.
But who wouldn't . . . look that age,
If they'd been around for more than a thousand decades.

Igor lived all alone,
He was nothing more than skin and bone.
His razor sharp teeth and pale lean face,
. . . I would never take his place.

Igor wasn't a companionable vampire,
Playing with him was like playing with fire.
Remember to carry garlic or a cross,
Without these two things you are surely lost.

As dawn arrived in Castle Dracula,
Which was right in the heart of Transylvania.
When sunlight hits any vampire alive,
Believe me they are sure to die.

Samre Kayani (13)
Southmoor Secondary School

How To Eat A Mars Bar

There's lots of different ways,
to eat a Mars bar.
It doesn't take much doing,
to eat it in your car.

You can eat it in batter,
you can eat it in a bun,
you can eat it for a laugh,
you can eat it for fun.

You can eat it in white,
and get it down your dress,
you can get it on your face,
and make a right mess.

You can get into trouble,
and even start to bubble.
You can lick it off your face
and every other place.
It can dribble down your legs,
it can run down your knees
but that's a Mars bar
so eat it how you please.

Jennifer Lugsden (12)
Southmoor Secondary School

A Hot Day

Sun shines
Children play
Sea roars
Fish swim
Seagulls scream
Mice scuttle
Bats hide
Streams glisten
Water runs
Ice-cream melts
Pop sparkles
Clouds hover
Rain falls
People run
Darkness falls
Night is here.

Luisa Dailey (13)
Southmoor Secondary School

Pigs, Pigs, Pigs

Pigs are quite adorable creatures,
Despite having such monstrous features,
Most people think of them as food on legs,
And a smell you can't cover up with pegs,
But as a vegetarian I think twice,
Before tucking into stir-fried pork and rice.
I'd rather have tofu and Quorn,
And let the sweet little porkers live on and on.

Ashleigh Clark (13)
Southmoor Secondary School

MY RABBIT FLUFF

My rabbit is Fluff
He runs joyfully happy in his run
On a night he comes into the house
He sits contentedly on my knee snugly and warm

His white fur is like silk to the touch
His nose is prickly and sensitive
His tongue is rough and hot
His ears hang loose, limp beside his delicate face

Still only young
His bright blue eyes follow every move you make
The big fat cat watches every move he makes
At the slightest noise he is alert

His playful moods, crazy hours
He sits preening himself
Licks his big ears and fluffy paws
Then lies down by the warm radiator
for a rest

That's my rabbit Fluff
Gorgeous petite and cute
Playful daft and dog-like
Yet always ready to lie down for a cuddle.

Philip Farley (13)
Southmoor Secondary School

MAMA - MY GREAT GRANDMA

I remember,
Her happy nature,
Her never-ending smile,
Never wanting to be alone.

I remember,
Her permed grey and white hair,
Her quite big build,
Eyes as big as footballs.

I remember,
The funeral day,
Everyone talking about her,
All good of course.

I remember,
Everyone called her mama,
She was like a mam to them.
She loved her worst enemy.

I remember,
Her love for her great-grandchildren.
Some of them knew her,
A lot more didn't.

Maybe someday they will see her,
Wherever she is right now.
But whether they do or not,
I hope I do!

Jennie Errington (13)
Southmoor Secondary School

THE GHOST

The eerie noises around the house,
the creaking of the floor.
My eyes closed tight with fear and fright.
I wait for it to go.

This unknown ghost,
my room its host,
to pace all through the night,
I can't move or make a sound,
no one to hear my plight.

Who it is, and where it's from
I will never know,
for I'm too scared to take a peep
in case its eyes my own might meet.

I wait for morning,
and as it's dawning,
the light floods in my room.
I know it's passed and so is my fear,
no more doom and gloom.

I've managed yet another night
in my haunted room.
I hope my ghost will go,
and I am hoping
very soon!

Vicky Toft (13)
Southmoor Secondary School

WITCHES

Are the stories make-believe or true?
You are probably pondering that question too,
Nobody knows if they are female or male
But you have probably all heard a bewitching tale.

Well wait until you hear mine,
It's guaranteed to send a shiver down your spine.

It takes place in a town called Crompton in the year 1686,
When witches were up to their evil tricks,
And anybody who was different or had a funny smell,
Was said to be a witch and was to be burned in Hell.

Now perched on a hill in Crompton town was a small house,
Infested with rats and the odd field mouse,
But inside was a creature more dreadful than a rat,
She had jet black hair and a beady-eyed cat.

You have probably guessed what she is,
The most wicked witch ever Devil Eyed Liz,
Her lips are fat and juicy red,
And she wears a small pointed hat upon her wicked head.

You would never see her during the day,
Oh no she likes to hide away,
Until the darkness hides all
And the howling wolves begin to call.

But she's not the type to fly on her broom,
She prefers to shout magic spells at the moon,
And think about who her next victim will be,
In this case the girl was called Sandy Lee.

Ha, little did she know that Sandy Lee,
Was a more powerful witch than she!
Wouldn't Devil Eyed Liz be in for a shock,
If she tried to turn Sandy Lee into a scaly croc.

But Devil Eyed Liz didn't have a clue
That her prey Sandy Lee was an evil witch too,
So when Liz tried to turn her into spider pie,
The clever Sandy Lee turned her into a fly.

Now the ending of my tale is plain to see,
Beware of anyone named Sandy Lee!

Emma Orwin (13)
Southmoor Secondary School

BIRDS OF PREY

Birds of prey are magnificent,
Roosting in trees,
Floating through the sky,
Rearing their young.
You wish you could:
Soar with the eagles,
Stalk with the raptors,
Glide with the kites,
Swoop with the falcons,
Hover with the hawks,
Hoot with the owls,
Pursue with the osprey,
Devour with the buzzards,
Hunt with the harriers,
Or scavenge with the vultures,
And you'll think,
It's all wonderful.

Martyn Smithson (13)
Southmoor Secondary School

A DAY ON THE STARSHIP VOYAGER

The crew beamed down to the planet Zorg
In search of some vital supplies,
Then came along the horrid Borg
And poked them in the eyes.

They started to assimilate
Transforming the crew in fives,
They ended up in such a state
I was surprised they were still alive!

They beamed back to the ship in shock
Taken straight to see the Doctor,
'Come on you guys,' he said like Spock
'Now sit down, Lt Proctor!'

The ship took off at warp 9.4
To escape the metal monsters,
But bumped into some unfriendly folk
The Minocratogronsters"

Paris steered away from them
To avoid their deadly ray,
But chipped the side of the Chronoflem
So all began to pray.

The ship spun round, the consoles blew
As the vessel headed for a planet,
The Captain screamed as she watched her crew
Get thrown onto the granite.

The bumpy landing shook the ship
And caused a lot of damage,
'Can we fix the problems, Skip?'
'Nothing we can't manage.'

The ship got fixed and then took off
And sped off through the stars,
'Where should we head?' asked Lt Tuvok
Destination: Mars!

Paul Green (13)
Southmoor Secondary School

HORRIS THE GNOME

Way up in the mountains,
Where the skies do groan,
Lived a funny little thing,
Called Horris the gnome.

He lived inside the mountain top,
In a deep, dark cave,
He had a long white beard,
As he couldn't really shave.

He was very small and stubborn,
And always seemed to shout,
He devoured so much every day,
And appeared rather stout.

So if you see old Horris,
Don't talk to him, just run,
Because if he finds you unawares,
He'll have you in his tum!

Christopher Carlin (13)
Southmoor Secondary School

DEEP IN THE JUNGLE

Deep in the jungle,
Tigers growl
Monkeys sway
Snakes slither
Crocodiles snap,
Parrots squawk
Giraffes gnaw
Panthers pant
Bees sting,
Mosquitoes munch
Lions prowl
Frogs leap
Spiders scuttle
Lizards lie,
All light fades
Darkness falls.

Rachael Hartis (13)
Southmoor Secondary School

FRIENDS

Friends are for life,
Or that's what they say,
They never treat you badly,
Never stray.

But once in a while,
All friendships go through a patch,
Where things are muttered,
That the other doesn't quite catch.

But if the friendship is strong enough,
To overcome those fights,
A special bond is ever made,
That will last your life.

And that is why,
If you treat your friends well and with care,
The friendship will blossom,
Into something to treasure and share.

Helen Kinmond (13)
Southmoor Secondary School

MY FRIEND

There was an alien who came from Mars,
He had the strange name of Mag.
He became my mate,
Though when we went out,
He got the date!

One dark night,
Walking home from school,
I had a huge fright,
I was beamed up high,
Into the dark, black sky.

It was Mag's spaceship of course,
To unpleasant tests I was the source.
Though meeting Mag made up for that,
Good friends we've been since then.
We go out every Friday night,
Then get back home for ten.

Christopher Wilson (13)
Southmoor Secondary School

THROUGH THE PARK

Waters ripple,
mice scuttle.

Raindrops drip,
bushes click.

Rivers run,
children having fun!

Streams glisten,
fish swimmin'.

Rain patters,
thunder clatters.

Grass waves,
dark caves.

Branches sway,
horses neigh.

Sunbeams light,
pretty kites.

What a lovely sight!

Sarah Richardson (13)
Southmoor Secondary School

TO YOU ON MOTHER'S DAY . . .

I was going to buy you a lovely card,
With hearts of pink and red,
But then I thought I'd rather spend the
Money on me instead.

It's really hard to buy things,
When one's pocket money is so small,
So I suppose you are pretty lucky
You got anything at all.

Happy Mother's Day to you,
There I said it and now I'm done,
So how about getting out of bed,
And cooking breakfast for your son.

Laura Carter (13)
Southmoor Secondary School

FOOTBALL AGAIN!

Whistle bellows
Ball kicked
Winger sprints
Forward strikes
Defenders slide
Tackles crunch
Keepers dive
Crowds chant
Ref shouts
Players yell
Fists thrown
Cards shown
Crowds boo
Penalty taken
Goal scored
Players celebrate
Anger rises
Whistle blows
Ball booted
Mid-fielders fly
Crowd sings
Match won
Champions again
Next year?
Football again!

Martin Forster (13)
Southmoor Secondary School

A RECIPE FOR LOVE

6kg of laughter
10kg of friendship
10kg of happiness
7kg of care
15kg of love
7kg of understanding
14kg of kindness
14kg of good looks
1 strand of hair
4 rose heads

Method

First mix 6kg of laughter until it bubbles.
Then add 10kg of friendship and happiness until it turns pink.
Next add a pinch of care.
15kg of love and 7 kg of understanding until red.
Then 4 rose heads and to finish it off 1 strand of hair
from the person you love and put it in a pot and keep it safe.

Amy Hurst (11)
Usworth Comprehensive School

SPELLS

A witch in a cape and a black pointed hat.
She always has with her,
her sleek black cat.
In the corner a cauldron bubbles,
strange words spoken as she stirs.
Around her legs, her black cat purrs.
The children fade back into the past.
The witch's spell has been well cast.

Sharrie Muter (11)
Usworth Comprehensive School

MYSTERY AND MAGIC

A witch stands in her kitchen
cutting up frogs and rats.
She puts them in the cauldron
to boil with dried up bats.

A secret spell that she is saying,
abracadabra and alakazam,
makes the cauldron bubble
and go kabam.

The whole house shakes,
even the snakes and rats and dried up bats.
The cauldron, the roof, the walls,
and the witch shoot up to space,
and that's the end to her mystery and magic.

Kevin Bestford (13)
Usworth Comprehensive School

NIGHT AND DAY

Why does the sun rise and set every day
Like a giant beach ball?
Why does the tide go in and out every night
Snaking up the sand, then sneaking back again.
Why do the stars wink at you every night
Like fairies hovering in the sky?
Why does the moon make faces at you?
Big blue circles on his face.
Why? Nobody knows, it's all mystery and magic.

Helen Syme (13)
Usworth Comprehensive School

THE INSTRUMENT

Behind a waterfall in a little room
which was hidden beneath a cave,
I found it.
I brushed away the dust of the years
and picked it up, holding it in my hands.
I had no idea what it was
but it was beautiful.

I put my fingers across the wires
and turned the keys to make it sound.
I struck the wires with my other hand
and produced my first harmonious sound.

See how it sings like a sad heart
and joyously screams out its pain.
Sounds that build high like a mountain
and notes that fall gently like rain.

Malcolm Nevins (13)
Usworth Comprehensive School

THE EARTH

How did the Earth begin?
Did it blow up like a balloon
or is it really rock?
God might have made it from clay
nobody really knows,
it's a mystery.
Where did all the things come from,
all the trees and grass and animals?
Nobody really knows because it's a mystery.

Amy Fletcher (13)
Usworth Comprehensive School

13 O'CLOCK

The clock struck thirteen
In the middle of the village green
The winds were blowing
The rivers stopped flowing
And bowed to the witches
of the night.

The bravest of creatures hid
As the witches did
A spell in which they said
All the children in bed
Would have a head made
of bread.

They began their song
And said the word *pong*
Eye of frog and head of rat
Then the end of a cricket bat
Went into the pot which
was red hot.

As they danced around
They found a magic pound
And wished the spell
Would not smell
And for it to come true and
not to be blue.

The spell became real
Such a terrible ordeal
All the children had bread
Instead of heads
Then the clock struck one and
everything was gone.

Rachael Gibson (11)
Usworth Comprehensive School

SPELLBOUND

They wait until the clock strikes twelve
And get the cauldron ready,
Little children lie in bed
Gripping tight their teddy.

The witches call a gathering
With wizards and with ghosts,
They fly around on broomsticks
And meddle with their hosts.

Why was the air so creepy?
Like someone was so near,
I could feel the breath upon my face
And the whisper in my ear.

Some lightning struck the aerial
And caused a massive bang,
The witches found their magic
And were dancing as they sang:
'Let the children have a nightmare
Like they never have had before.'
But when little Amy woke up
She was floating off the floor.

All of the cats guarded the children
To make sure they'll never wake,
And the cats will be rewarded
With a big fat juicy steak.

Danielle Fairweather (11)
Usworth Comprehensive School

THE MAGICIAN

A magical stick
A dream come true
A mysterious wonderland
For me and you.

The curtains open
All wonders to see
Magic words spoken
A child laughs in glee.

A floating ball
How does he do that?
A dove to appear
A rabbit from his hat.

The show is now over
The applause is so great
A bow from the magician
For his next show we'll have to wait.

Joanne Bainbridge (13)
Usworth Comprehensive School

ENCHANTED

Enchanted woods at the end of the gate,
No one stays out there very late,
'Cause if they do, the magic will
have them for the victim of its next kill.
And then the bodies will be kept,
Noon every day they will be swept,
Until the day they rot away.
Evil in the woods will always stay,
Down in the deep, dark woods.

Kayleigh Ingham (11)
Usworth Comprehensive School

A Lost Paradise!

Far, far away from home,
To a magical place,
To a place unknown,
Unknown to woman, man or child
A place that's different,
A place that's wild,
With overgrown forests and bushes and trees,
The sun shining bright, with a slight swirling breeze,
And only the creatures, that crawl down below,
And the wasps and the bees that can only show,
How much of a wonderland,
That nobody knows,
How much of a dreamland,
Where nobody goes.

Joanne Quigley (14)
Usworth Comprehensive School

Mystery And Magic

I saw a pretty flower.
Whatever could it be?
'It's an animal' they said
'a sea anemone.'

I saw a fish in armour
it had a very long snout.
They said it was a sea horse,
firmly, without any doubt.

I recognised a garden plant
upon the ocean bed.
'No that's a sea cucumber
a marine animal' they said.

Vicky Litster (13)
Usworth Comprehensive School

The Voices

He came late at night,
And knocked on the door.
'Open up,' he said, 'I'm cold and sore
No answer came from inside the place
Though someone looked out and saw his face

The man was old and thin and tired,
He only wanted to sleep inside.
'Go away,' a voice replied
'All who have stayed here have died.'

'I just need a bed,' the man cried out
'Let me in and have no doubt,
I will leave first thing next morning
Just as the early sun is dawning.'

'I'll let you in,' said the voice
'For, of course, I have no choice,
But listen to what I have said
Tomorrow morning you'll be dead.'
The man laughed to himself and stepped inside
That voice is small and sweet and kind.

'Do not laugh sir my voice is kind,
The cruel voices are in my mind
They only ever call at night,
To seal a traveller's unknown plight.'
The man smiled and rubbed his head,
Undressed and then got into bed.

The next day the small girl found,
His body lying on the ground.
'I warned him,' she said 'more than twice
They always think that I'm nice.
Why does this happen?' the child cried,
'You'll never know,' her head replied.

Kathryn Sawyers (13)
Usworth Comprehensive School

THE WITCH

I had a dream
  A dream had I
    About a tall white lady
      With long black hair

She had a wart on her nose
  Pointed fingers, pointed toes
    A tall black hat
      And a long black coat

She sat all day long
  On a stool making spells
    Like an old cranky woman
      Till the very end

She reads out the spells
  And the mixtures in between
    Shouting the ingredients
      That we would never eat ourselves

A toad's nose
  A kitten's eye
    A wing of a bat
      And the postman's hat
        A tail of a newt
          A spider's web
            Mixing every ingredient as she said

All of a sudden
  A cloud of smoke filled the air
    I looked over to the door
      The witch was no longer there

Then as my dream ended
  And everything went black
    I heard a shout from my mum saying
      'Gillian you're late.'

Gillian Stewart (13)
Usworth Comprehensive School

HOOVES ON THE ICY ROAD

Walking home one dark foggy night,
Everything was still.
My breath hung on the air.
Steadily I walked,
Out of the darkness
A sound, faint, I heard.
It came closer, closer.
Horses' hooves on the icy road,
I stepped to one side to let them pass,
Wondering why should they be out
On such a cold, dark night.
The noise got louder,
I turned and looked for them
But no one or nothing was there.
The sound went past.
I shrank back into the hedge,
Holding my breath with fear.
Into the fog the hoof-beats went
But nothing had gone past me.

Scott Brown (13)
Usworth Comprehensive School

WEST-MOOR ESTATE!

There's always something going on,
On the corner of West-Moor Estate,
Don't worry that you'll not see it,
'Coz you're never too early or late!

I walked round there yesterday
Roughly about eight-thirty-three,
It was just about then I noticed,
There was a man walking over to me.

I didn't think anything of it,
But when I caught the glimpse in his eyes,
I knew practically straight away
I was in for big surprise!

When I walked in his direction again
The man that had been standing near
Had deceived my eyes amazingly,
For my eyes just saw him disappear!

Victoria Kirtley (13)
Usworth Comprehensive School

ILLUSIONS

The scene was set, the lights were low,
He dressed in black from head to toe.
He stepped inside a box of blue
The people did not have a clue.

The drape rose up above his head,
All went dark then there was a flash of red.
The drape fell down and there was a gasp
Because he was a she and the crowd couldn't grasp.

Where had the first disappeared to,
I didn't know and neither would you.
There from the side the first man came in
And the crowd erupted with a thunderous din.

Nicholas Bell (13)
Usworth Comprehensive School

QUEEN OF HEARTS

It will always be a mystery,
of why God took Diana's short life from us.
She was a beautiful and caring person,
at the age of 36.
It has shown to the world,
that this has been an awful loss.
Her sons have proven,
that they are the bravest of the brave.
Diana lost her love, Dodi, too
in this tragic event.
They were about to marry,
but died all too soon.
The funeral has been the saddest part,
the songs, the sermon and the sad truth.
But through all of this,
she will remain with us forever
and will always be our Queen of Hearts.

Lucy Barber (13)
Usworth Comprehensive School

MYSTERY AND MAGIC

Life is a mystery to me
Why do fish swim in the sea?
How many tea bags make the perfect cup of tea?
How many feet are in a mile?
Could I make Mona Lisa smile?
It's a mystery to me.

How many marshmallows can I cram in my mouth?
Why is north, north and why is south, south?
Why with food mountains piled so high
Do little children starve and die?
It's a mystery to me.

Why do people drink and drive
When each time they risk someone's life?
Why are my socks under my bed
And not in my chest of drawers instead?
It's a mystery to me.

Adam Dixon (13)
Usworth Comprehensive School

MYSTERY AND MAGIC

Is magic a mystery
Is the mystery really the magic for sure
Magic is not real magic
But for sure
Magic is really magical
Is that the mystery
The mystery of magic.

Sara Lang (13)
Usworth Comprehensive School

THE MAGICIAN

The boy looked quickly,
Music played louder and louder,
A flash, a bang, a roll of drums,
And there they were.

There was nothing at all in the box,
Only the swords going through it,
A large box, with golden locks,
And lines with a golden cloth.

The lights grew dim quickly,
He said his magic words,
And waved his arms all over,
Lights flashed and the music played.

The audience watched in amazement,
The 'oohs' and 'aahs' could be heard,
The assistant rose out of the box,
To stand and bow to the applause.

And just as quickly as she appeared,
Smoke rose and covered the stage,
He waved his cloak all over,
And in a minute she was gone again.

The magician waved his arms again,
Withdrew the swords once more,
He opened the box slowly,
Leaned over to pick something up.

The 'oohs' and 'aahs' were heard again,
And a puppy yelped with glee,
What happened to the lady?
No one knows - only he.

Suzanne Cook (13)
Usworth Comprehensive School

THE MAGICIAN

The magician's magical mayhem and mirth,
Was never really quite
Down to earth.
His owl named Dell
Helped out with his spells
And the commotion was out
Of control.
He turned cows into frogs,
Cats into dogs and tried to
Turn lead into gold.
He slew dragons and witches, ogres
and goblins,
He really was quite bold!
But then one day he met his end,
From a cannibal giant
He tried to defend.
It rubbed its tum and pointed in glee and the
Magical wizard cried
'I'm not food, it's me!
It's me!'
But the cannibal giant,
A greedy lad, devoured the
Wizard and said 'Just too bad.'

Gary Routledge (13)
Usworth Comprehensive School

SPELLBOUND

On a dark night
On a dark hill
In a dark cauldron
Brewed a dark liquid
A wizard brooded over it
Stoking the fire
Adding things
Stirring it
He added a gold powder
Then *bang!*
A gigantic monstrous fiend
Appeared before his eyes.
A gruesome sight
Purple eyes
Green skin
Bright orange hair and a string vest,
Boxer shorts,
Three arms, six legs, one eye.
With a sudden flash and bang
The wizard threw a potion at the monster
And the monster disappeared
Into the magic book of spells.
Looks like he's *spellbound!*

Kayleigh Underwood (11)
Usworth Comprehensive School

SPELLBOUND

Teenage years
Up the stairs
In the room
Music;
Boom!
Playing loud
Moaning sound
Think he's lush
Have a crush
Him 'n' me
In a tree
That's the song -
Oh no! What's wrong?
Homework to do
Have no clue.
In comes Mam.
Door,
Slam!
'Have you had drugs,
Been planning mugs?'
It's down the sink
With what they think!
Go back to school
Where teachers rule!
It's that lad
He's been bad
But he denies;
With rolling eyes
Smurky grin
Spotty chin.

Miss Western School
(Who thinks she's cool)
Enters the room -
I spoke too soon
Dirty look
She treats me like a piece of muck!
I wring my thumbs
'cos here he comes.
Oh, it's him!
I glance to give my loving grin.
Go back home,
Home alone.
Up the stairs
In the room
Music,
Boom!

Laura Bertram (12)
Western Middle School

SPELLBOUND

An unbelievable feeling,
Unexplainable,
A mixture of excitement and fascination,
Spellbound.

Under a spell,
Cannot escape,
Trapped, uncomfortable, scared,
Spellbound.

Witches round a cauldron,
Mixing a potion,
Getting ready to make someone
Spellbound.

Two different meanings,
Fascination or under a spell
A wonderful word,
Spellbound.

Jessica Fairs (10)
Western Middle School

SPELLBOUND

Silence and darkness!
Sitting out in space,
Without the lights
Shining on me.

Little twinkles of light
Start to come out
From hiding.
Everything is quiet.

The stars are so small
From where I am,
Sitting out in space,
I feel spellbound.

The stars are so far away.
But I think I can
Just feel them.
Little twinkles of light
Are fully out.
I feel spellbound.

Katy Barron (11)
Western Middle School

SPELLBOUND

A chaotic scramble
of words
and pictures.
In enchanted dreams
and thoughts
where
time and space
don't exist and
a mixture of
fiery passion and a
whirl of
Hocus pocus
collide
with your
emotions
to combine confusion
and an
overwhelming
sense of
bewilderment
where
silence screams
into your ears
and crawls
into your brain
to leave you
speechless
yet with
a thousand things
to say.

Spellbound . . .

Mel McCartney (12)
Western Middle School

THINGS I HAVE LOVED

These I have loved:
I like to see the dog playing in the garden,
like an excited lion, playing with its ball.

The touch of a horse's nose
reminds me of a soft sponge.

I like to see the birds singing
in the treetops, peaceful and calm.

The taste of chicken,
soft, chewy and smooth.

I like to feel the hot sun and
gentle wind on my face.

It makes me feel all hot and tingly.

All these things I still love.

Deborah Philpot (11)
Whitburn Comprehensive School

THE THINGS I LOVE

I love to smell bacon frying in a pan
and cold fresh air.

I love to feel a kitten's and puppy's fur so soft,
and dry soft sand running through toes and fingers.

I love to see my house from the top of the
street on a dark night with all the lights on.

All these have been my love.

Stacey Judd (11)
Whitburn Comprehensive School

THE GREAT LOVES

These I have loved:
      Long strips of spaghetti,
makes me go aah.
The strong taste of the browny bolognaise,
makes me go all light headed.
Chocolate, as it melts on my tongue,
The taste is unbelievable.
It reminds me of a long, bumpy road,
As it never seems to end!
I smell different smells,
But the one I love is the fresh smell of an orange,
I think the colour and size,
Is like the sky in the morning.
As I walk past my cat,
I think of soft dreamy clouds,
The fur makes me dreamy.
Snowflakes as they fall on my cheeks,
Make me feel as cold as gravestones.
I see things I don't like:
Spiders, beetles.
I see other things as well,
Ill people and poor people.
Then I see Newcastle United win,
Wildlife and bears.
As I wake from my dreamy sleep,
I hear the birds singing their cheery songs,
Which reminds me of a countryside.

I remember the good times I shared with a friend,
The laughs we shared together,
Come crawling back to me,
Then there were the sad things,
The sorrows we shared,
Out of the blue there I was,
Upset, afraid.
It never seemed to end.

Hannah Forster (11)
Whitburn Comprehensive School

MY FAVOURITE THINGS

These I have loved:
The touch of velvet, smooth, soft from the moment
I set down my hand
The sound of birds tweeting in the trees. This I love so much
The warm taste of cakes just out of the oven melting in my mouth
The look of stars gleaming brightly in the sky
The wind, I hate, so cold it gives me the shivers
I love the sound of brown autumn leaves crunching beneath my feet
The strong beam of the sun, so warm I feel like pouring
cool water over me
Crackling lightning brightens up the sky; blue,
white and yellow - *crash!*
The roar of thunder like a lion in the grasslands, scaring small
children into their homes
Flying through the clouds like a bird in the sky, looking down
on the ground through a window
Slimy worms I hate to feel, squirming and slithering
through my fingers.

Jeanette Richardson (11)
Whitburn Comprehensive School

THINGS I LOVE

In my mind
What makes a wonderful spell,
Is really the homely smell
Of coffee, and bacon that's frying.

I really love looking
At the sun setting over the hills,
And when I'm in the countryside, looking at windmills!

The smooth, rippling touch
Of silk, which I love so much
And the clean, firm, cooling feel of glass.

While the taste of fresh bread,
Fills my head,
With lots of wonderful thoughts!

Cheryl Arrowsmith (11)
Whitburn Comprehensive School

AUTUMN

I step outside to hear the sound of the crispy leaves beneath
my feet
and struck by the smell of a burning fire near,
now I know autumn is here.

Hedgehogs hibernate as the hedgerows turn brown.
This now makes me believe
autumn is here.

Danielle Collins (12)
Whitburn Comprehensive School

THINGS I HAVE LOVED

The smell of freshly baked bread drifts down the hallway
And as the radio blasts,
the soft fur of a kitten brushes past my legs.

> The creamy silkiness of white chocolate
> Covers the scrumptious red strawberries.
> Then the snap crackle pop of fireworks
> Lightens up the sky. People smile as they watch.

The smell of new carpet all clean and gleaming.
The sound of birds awakens me on a cold snowy day.
Outside the snow, no footprints just perfect.

> All of these have been
> my loves.

Laura Graham (11)
Whitburn Comprehensive School

THE THINGS I LOVE

These I have loved:
The smell of crispy, golden brown toast,
And the drifting aroma of spicy, hot curry.
The white crispy feel and sight of snow covering the ground,
The sensation of being the first to walk onto that clear white sheet.
The sound of a river flowing downstream,
And the tinkling of bells at Christmas time.
The sight of a present on your birthday, waiting to be unwrapped.
I love the tender touch of a ball of cotton wool,
And the fantastic feel of fur, rubbing against my skin.
All these are my loves.

Andrew Landsbury (12)
Whitburn Comprehensive School

THINGS I LOVE

Warm sand spreading between my feet on a breezy day
Sun setting on the sea, rainbows brightening a heavy sky,
Melon, sweet and juicy in a mountain of fruit,
The dusty smell of horses as I go and say hello
The sweet singing of birds as I wake up in the morning
Heavy rain crashing on the window, snow with no footprints.

A field of daffodils, swaying in the wind
The fragrance of a big white rose blooming in a garden
The delight of seeing the first white snowflake
The warmth of an open fire on a winter's night
Chocolate melting in my mouth, fireworks flying in the sky
Christmas trees at Christmas time
Christmas trees at Christmas time in windows as you walk past.

Amy Pattison (12)
Whitburn Comprehensive School

WHAT I LOVE!

My dear loves,
        The smell of petrol from a petrol pump, and a hot, roasted
chicken on a Sunday lunchtime. Sweet icing sugar on top of a soft
sponge cake and the sound of the rustling of leaves when people
trample all over them.
The snap, crackle and pop of rice crispies on a hot summer's morning,
the sound of oars ripping across the sea's surface. The feeling of
having a long rest after playing football.
The sound of a stapler clicking on some cardboard, also magazine pages
sliding on to the next page.
The crumbly taste of Fray Bentos pies, lying in my bed while the
rain's pouring down in winter.

Jonathan Cockburn (11)
Whitburn Comprehensive School

MY LOVES

These I have loved,
The crunching of dead leaves under my shoes that have
just dropped to the ground on a cold autumn morning.
The lashing of cool air on my face as I open the door
to the freezer and the feeling of nice fresh clean bedclothes
brushing against my body as I jump into bed.
Warm blasts of air down my neck as I sit next to the fire
on a winter's night, and the smell of a fire burning,
sending fumes of smoke up my nose on bonfire night.
The sight of the sun breaking through the clouds lighting up the sky
on a dull day.
The sound of rain beating on my window, as I lie snug in bed.
These I have loved and I still do.

Iain Fisher (11)
Whitburn Comprehensive School

THINGS I LOVE

I love:
        To taste the smooth milky chocolate melting in my mouth,
And I like to see the clear white snow without any footprints in.
I like to feel the fluffy fur on a teddy bear,
And the smell of dusty horse's as I walk through the farm.

The sweet taste of sweetcorn with melted butter,
And the sound of people enjoying themselves,
And the smell of a Sunday's dinner's gravy bubbling in the pan,
I like to taste the runny treacle on a pudding.

Amanda Owen (11)
Whitburn Comprehensive School

MY FAVOURITE THINGS

These I have loved:
        Ice-cream frozen like a mountain peak,
That tingly feeling on my tongue;
Apples juicy on my tongue,
Like a river running, the bright colours,
Red and green;
Chocolate melting slowly,
That lovely warm feeling inside;
The fresh smell of pine trees,
All out in the country, growing free;
That strong smell of petrol,
As my mum fills up with fuel;
The smell of white musk,
The sweet smelling perfume;
I love to stroke shaggy dogs,
With their fur tickling my fingers;
My favourite clothes,
With that smooth silk feel;
The smooth grainy feeling of sand,
Running through my fingers like water;
The sight of happy faces, with rosy red cheeks,
And smiles from ear to ear;
The bright shining colours, like the orange sunshine's rays,
Of yellow and green, to brighten up the days;
The early morning chirp, that wakes you up at dawn,
Sung by the birds is their happy bouncy song;
When you stroke a sweet cat,
Her ever so quiet purr is so grateful;
Down by the sea I hear the waves *splash!*
Crash! As they hit the rocks;
Watching films, going to the pictures with friends,
These I do enjoy;
When my dad comes home,
And family gatherings do make me happy;

But when my dad goes back to sea,
And dearest pets die,
I am upset;
The roar of the crowd, tension running,
All the hype of a football game,
But one side always has to come away gloomy,
And that's me when Newcastle are beaten;
These have been my loves.

Kayleigh Grainger (11)
Whitburn Comprehensive School

THINGS I HAVE LOVED

I love to see a new born baby trying to smile at me
And oh of course I have to say I love my new TV.
Yorkshire puddings have got to be my favourite so far
I can smell the strong scrumptious smell when I get out of my car.

When I go to my friend's house I love the sound of the
animals making the sound they do.
They moo, they oink, they neigh, and do different wonderful sounds.

I love the feel of my dog's fur and the nice silky feel of my new skirt.
And the great feel on my new carpet going up the stairs.

When I stop running up and down on the stairs there's a nice plate
of pizza waiting for me.
Then I go outside and smell the sweet fresh air.

All these I love.

Hayley Robson (11)
Whitburn Comprehensive School

THE THINGS I LOVE

The smell of the Christmas pudding having the alcohol
poured onto it and being set on fire.
And the salty vinegary smell when you walk into a fish and chip shop.

The sound of standing on fallen leaves in autumn
And the sound of Oasis' music playing on my CD player.

The feel of hot, soft fluffy towels, when you come out of the bath
And the feel of wet sand on your feet on a hot day at the beach.

The sight of freshly fallen snow with no footprints in
and the sun shining,
And the sight of sunset over the sea at dawn.

The taste of freshly grilled burgers straight off the barbecue
in mid-summer,
And the taste of a peach with the fur rubbing your lips.

Michael Jude (11)
Whitburn Comprehensive School

THINGS I LOVE

I love the irresistible aroma of honey
I love the smell of a hot meal on a cold afternoon.
I love the taste of my mum's sweet apple pie.
I love the taste of chocolate melting slowly in my mouth,
I love the salty wet feel of the sea spray,
I love the feel of getting into bed with nice clean soft sheets,
I love to see cheerful happy faces on Christmas Day,
I love to see the waves crashing against the cliffs,
I love to hear the hometime bell.

Kyle Atkinson (11)
Whitburn Comprehensive School

SEASONS

Blossom petals fall on the ground
Birds are flying all around
The nights and mornings are getting lighter
The flowers in the park are getting brighter.

Summer days are usually hot
To cool us down we eat ice-cream a lot
Some people lie all day in the sun
We play in the sand and have lots of fun.

The autumn months bring strong gales
Mostly rain and sometimes hail;
The ground is covered in many leaves
The leaves have fallen from the trees.

The gleaming frost on the roads at night
The ice covered lake is gleaming white
The streets are covered in ice and snow
The moon gives off a warmful glow.

Paul Renno (12)
Whitburn Comprehensive School

THINGS I LOVE

I love the smell of fresh mackerel in the morning
and fresh curry at night.
I love to touch wet sand and dog fur.
I love the sound of peacocks shouting and cockerels crowing.
I love the sight of the open countryside in the morning
and flocks of geese flying overhead.

Tyler Gibson (11)
Whitburn Comprehensive School

SEASONS OF SENSES

Seeing the sun sparkling in the early morning summer sunlight,
The juicy, tender taste of a succulent hot roast beef sandwich
on a frosty winter night.
The smoky wood smell of our clothes after the autumn bonfire.
Snuggling up to my soft furry Dalmatian whilst watching
the springtime blossom trees swaying.
Listening to the dawn chorus of the countryside before the
hustle and bustle of the cars.
I love all these seasons of senses.

I enjoy the sweet smell of crispy green apples as they bubble away
in the pan for autumn pies.
Watching my stunt kite soaring, swooping, looping the loop
on a windy March afternoon.
The rich, sweet taste of warm, sticky, melting Mars bars from the
smoky barbecue in summer.
The rustling sound of footsteps through crunchy autumn leaves.
I enjoy the soft smooth delicate feel of silk ties all on display.
I love all these seasons of senses.

Amy Hetherington (11)
Whitburn Comprehensive School

THINGS I LOVE

I like the sound of hot fire burning and crackling,
I love the smell of freshly baked bread,
I like to feel a warm blanket at bedtime,
The sound of a clock ticking in my head,
The sight of the beach with the sun turning red
and birds flying south,
The nice taste of chocolate in my mouth.

Victoria Laws (11)
Whitburn Comprehensive School

MY LOVES

I like the taste of:
Mints, spicy and sweet and,
Apples juicy and cold.
I adore the smell of
Petrol strong and leady and
The Sunday roast bubbling and hot.
I enjoy the sound of
Rain splashing on the roof at night, and
Rollercoaster cogs going round and round.
I love the sight of,
Ponds with fish swimming and hiding and
Rabbits hopping and bouncing.
I love the feelings of,
Rubber soft and stretchy and
Quilts, warm and soft.
I cherish,
Coal fires, warm and bright and
Fireworks banging and crackling.

Stuart Dobson (11)
Whitburn Comprehensive School

THINGS I LOVE

I love the taste of home-made gravy, on a Christmas dinner,
The smell of Yorkshire puddings is a delight.
I love the feel of sand rushing through my fingers,
The cheers of excitement when Newcastle score.
I love the sight of fireworks on Guy Fawkes night, light up the sky,
The salty, vinegary taste of fish 'n' chips warms up my mouth.

Ian Jones (11)
Whitburn Comprehensive School

THINGS I LOVE

I love,
The smell of freshly baked bread, hot from the oven,
floured and crisp,
The taste of fluffy meringues with crisp edges,
soft and delicate to the touch.
I like to see golden sunsets in a dark and cloudy sky,
The sound of crackling of an open fire on a rainy night.
I like to hear the thundery sound of the waves crashing on the shore,
The feel of soft and silky hamster fur.
I love the sweet sensation of milky hot chocolate on a cold day,
I love the sight of a clear rainbow just after rainfall.
I love the warm greasy taste of chips as I walk along the shore.
I love the feel of the cold waves cooling my feet,
I love the sight of first snowfall in winter.

Samantha Leask (12)
Whitburn Comprehensive School

WINTER

The trees are bare,
And the birds have gone,
The winter season has finally come
The clouds are full of winter snow
And people wear their woolly clothes
The feeling of our merry Christmas
Will bring those kids through happiness!

Amanda Hussain (12)
Whitburn Comprehensive School

A COLD WINTER NIGHT

One more winter has arrived
for now the animals cannot survive.
They dig and hide and live in burrows
where the wind cannot follow.

For some are not as lucky as them
they search and seek but cannot fend
against the cold winter night
which gives the animals such a fright.

The end of winter has come at last
the animals are glad it's passed.
And now the robin and bluebirds sing
and give out an almighty ring.

Ryan Williams (12)
Whitburn Comprehensive School

JACK FROST

Today is winter, and we all know what this means,
Jack Frost is on his way.
Turns boys into snowballing machines,
He freezes everything he sees,
Bushes from green to white,
Leaves all frozen and crisp,
The path is slippery and cold,
Ponds turn to giant ice-cubes,
And works through the night,
And freezes what he can,
Sooner or later the summer does come,
And saves us,
But he will be back next winter.

Nicholas O'Brien (12)
Whitburn Comprehensive School

THINGS I LOVE

I love,
The warming taste of hot chips as I walk along the beach,
The smoky burning aroma of wood on a bonfire,
The loving feel of a big cuddle when I come in from school.
The thundering sound of the sea as it crashes on the rocks,
The excitement of seeing the first snowfall on the ground in winter,
The loud, crackling of fireworks as they light up the sky,
The smooth taste of lemon sorbet as it melts in your mouth,
The sensational smell of pancakes floating down the hall,
The kind, caring feel of my warm coat on a cold winter's day,
And the sweet chirping sound of birds singing as I wake in the morning.

I love,
The refreshing smell of seaweed as I stroll along the beach,
The sweet and sour taste of my nana's famous apple pie.
The sight of full beaches, on the summer's hottest days,
The relaxing feel of hot water, which massages as I step into the bath.
Snowball fights in the street, bringing out everybody's young side,
That shiver down your spine which fills you with excitement
on Christmas Eve.
The tempting sight of all the lovely clothes in the shop windows,
The satin feel of a rose petal and the gorgeous fragrance they give,
The smooth, soft smell of babies as I walk into a baby's room,
Or the smooth, soft feel of a puppy or kitten's fur coat,
And the unexplainable feeling of being on stage, acting in a show.

Rachel Hedley (11)
Whitburn Comprehensive School

MY FAVOURITE THINGS

These I have loved:
The shimmering, shining sea as the sun rises.
My cat pouncing, playing in the moonlight.
The sound of waves crashing on the shore.
Birds singing sweetly, happily.
My cat purring after a good meal.
Running my fingers through my dog's velvety fur coat;
The delicious smell of dinner cooking.
Early morning dew, so fresh and crisp.
Ice-cream, cakes and Coca-Cola are all so delicious, tasty and gorgeous.
Most of all I like to go to the beach and see the sea, or
to the Wildfowl Park to feed the delightful birds.

Melanie Seward (11)
Whitburn Comprehensive School

MY FEELINGS

These I have loved:
Soft fudge on a cold winter's day melting in my mouth,
People smiling, lightning in the bright night sky,
Soft fur of animals, silk rubbing against my skin,
The sweet scent of flowers, perfume, the fragrant smells
of pot-pourri,
Laughter, thunder and loud music tingle in my ears,
Learning to ride a bike, smiling with happiness,
Pain shot through me spraining my ankle,
Tears trickling down my face like raindrops,
The death of my rabbit slow and harsh.

Louise Richardson (11)
Whitburn Comprehensive School

THESE I HAVE LOVED

(Dedicated to the teachers at the Dyslexia Institute in Jesmond)

Biking on the Leas, very, very fast.
All the different greens, with my friends cheering me on.

Pavlovas crunchy and white, soft cream,
it makes your mouth water with those smells.
The fruits all different colours, the red of the strawberries,
the yellow of the mangoes, the green of the kiwi.

Spiders make some people itch but I like them.
Spiders' webs are like a net, just waiting for an innocent victim.

I love board games because of the thrill and a chance of winning,
being with all the people, the atmosphere.

I love walking in the country with the dogs and watching wildlife.

David James Wolfe (12)
Whitburn Comprehensive School

AUTUMN DAYS

The birds are gone, they've flown away
To a warmer climate and there they will stay,
Until winter is over and summer arrives,
So they can carry on with their lives.
The blue skies have gone and the grey ones have come,
The dull days are here and we all think the same,
That we have this weather yet it brings us together,
(When we huddle around the fire)
The leaves on the trees are crusty and old,
They lie on the ground brown, orange and gold.

Andrea Baxter (12)
Whitburn Comprehensive School

MY FAVOURITE THINGS

I love the gorgeous sweet taste of Cadbury's milk chocolate,
Tasting fresh juicy melon sliced on a plate,
The strange aromatic smell of burning wood,
The warm welcoming smell of roasting food.

I love the sharp crisp sound of paper as it is torn,
And the sound of the cold north wind as it whistles
on a cold autumn morn.
The sight of fresh white snow all light and fluffy,
And the sight of the huge winter waves crashing in
As if the sea was very huffy.

I love the feel of soft squishy Play-doh,
And my soft fluffy blanket as it warms me so.
The feel of clean crisp sheets as I climb into bed,
And driving through a dark blanket of trees
As they cast shadows over my head.

Sarah Duncan (11)
Whitburn Comprehensive School

AUTUMN

The leaves are falling from the trees,
No longer are there bumble bees.
The birds have long flown far away,
To hotter countries for many a day.

The birds no longer do they sing,
And gone is the happiness that they bring.
Warm coats, keep all the children warm,
And shield them against the fierce storm.

Gemma Backhouse (12)
Whitburn Comprehensive School

WINTER

First the ice cold wind arrives.
It is ice cold and sharp like glass.
Then the feather like snowflakes fall
And whiten the luscious green grass.

Then comes the end of the snowy showers
And the hills and slopes are littered with thrills.
The boys and girls sledge there for hours.
Then they return home all covered in chills.

Now the winter fades away, the
stalks and buds begin to bloom.
Spring is just around the corner,
It will be warm and glistening soon.

John Edgar (13)
Whitburn Comprehensive School

SEASON POEM

S pring is warm but sometimes rains
P aper floats down the back lanes
R agged leaves fall off trees
I n spring you always sing
N o one out in the street
G one inside to warm their feet.

S plendid sunshine all day long
U nder the trees we all cool down
M ay days are here with bright blue flowers
M any birds fly around the bright blue sky
E veryone playing with happiness
R eally enjoying themselves and happily playing all day long.

Dean Finch (12)
Whitburn Comprehensive School

WINTER POEM

The snow flutters down
And lands on the ground
Everything is covered
So nothing can be found

I look out of the window
Everything is white
The birds can't see any food
So they have taken flight

All you can hear is crunching
As I walk through the snow
All the land is covered
You can't see anything grow

There's not a footprint to be seen
Not a single one
Then someone comes and disturbs the snow
And the pretty scene has gone.

Katie Palmer (12)
Whitburn Comprehensive School

SUMMER

S ummer sun shines brightly
U pon the hills on an afternoon
M y family and I have a picnic
M any butterflies flutter by
E ach one a different colour
R ed roses grow in abundance.

Louise Lumsdon (12)
Whitburn Comprehensive School

THE FOUR SEASONS

It's spring, it's spring
It's spring again
Baby lambs have been born
Baby chicks for us to see
It's springtime again.

It's summer, it's summer
It's summer again
Holiday time and red hot sun
Making life all fun, fun, fun!
It's summer time again

It's autumn, it's autumn
It's autumn again
Harvest time is here
Gathering and stacking all the hay
It's autumn time again.

It's winter, it's winter
It's winter again
Although you don't see very much sun
Winter time can be great fun.
It's winter time again.

Stacey Hobson (12)
Whitburn Comprehensive School

THINGS I LOVE

I really love the taste of cold ice-cream,
with the sweet smell of flowers close by.
I also love the sound of water trickling into a pond
and the sound of little birds singing in the trees
and the taste of chocolate too.

Laura Hanson (12)
Whitburn Comprehensive School

THINGS THAT I LOVE

The taste of glorious juicy melon on a hot summer's day,
To hear the howling wind whistle down the chimney,
Feeling a thick warm blanket wrapped round me
on a cold night in winter,
Smelling pine from a new Christmas tree,
The sight of fresh crisp gleaming white snow,
Going for a drive in the country, through a tunnel
of towering green tree.

The taste of steaming hot chocolate on a cold winter's night,
Smelling freshly cut bright green grass,
Hearing the autumn multi-coloured leaves crunching underfoot,
The feel of someone playing with my hair,
Curling up in front of the fire on a cold night,
Going down to the beach at high tide and seeing the waves
crashing up the cliffs.

Katherine Burn (12)
Whitburn Comprehensive School

AN AUTUMN POEM

Leaves falling off the trees
Quiet buzzing of tired bees
Flowers disappear in the garden one by one.
Birds are ready to be gone, gone, gone
To warmer climates, for the winter's coming.
Rain and sleet on my windows drumming
The days are shorter the nights are long
Now that autumn's come along.

Stefanie De Giorgio (12)
Whitburn Comprehensive School

THESE I HAVE LOVED

The delicious taste of pizza which makes your mouth water
The cheese and the crust which run past your teeth
The smooth taste of chocolate ice-cream melting down your throat.

The crispy taste of chips, which crunches your teeth.
Smells of red roses make you nice and fresh.
And the smell of curry making you eat it all up.

Feeling of someone caring for me like my mama's hand touching me,
Seeing the beautiful blue sky changing shape to shape,
I remember when I was looking at the sea

Which reminded me that I am all free
When I look down as if I'm having a summer night's dream
As I am flying I can hear the children playing

The traffic was congesting on all routes
I am lucky that I am flying high up in the sky
No one tells me to turn left or right.

Shahbaz Ali (12)
Whitburn Comprehensive School

AUTUMN DAYS

Autumn days are the best,
It is here at last,
Leaves falling to the ground,
I don't want to see it pass,
Crispy leaves red and orange,
The crunchy sound under my feet,
I love the autumn days.

Kelly Ramm (12)
Whitburn Comprehensive School

THING I LOVE

In autumn time I love:
the crunchy leaves,
cool crisp air.
In spring I love
the pollen grains
and a buzz of a bee.
In winter time I love
the frost on the windows,
fire logs crackling and
me in my bed
like a bug in a rug.
The smell of freshly
baked apple pie.

Tina Clark (11)
Whitburn Comprehensive School

SPRING

When you hear little chicks sing;
Then you know it's the start of spring.
In spring we smell blooming flowers,
We see the last of the April showers,
When we smell fresh cut grass,
We know winter weather will pass,
Seeing little lambs playing,
And the flowers in the meadow swaying,
Then we hope spring is staying,
When you don't hear chicks sing;
That's when it's the end of spring.

Jennifer O'Neill (12)
Whitburn Comprehensive School

A SEASONAL POEM

Autumn
The leaves are coloured
The wind is strong
The clouds are clear
The leaves are always near

Winter
Winter's coming
Children playing
The snow is falling
Santa's calling

Spring
The flowers begin to bloom
The birds begin to sing
The cold winter's passed
Now it's spring again.

Summer
Summertime is here
The holiday time is near
The buckets and spades are out
Ready for the sun coming out.

Gemma Carr (12)
Whitburn Comprehensive School

THINGS I LOVE

A ruby red sunset vanished over a hill
And the beautiful sound of a nightingale.

The sound of the chug as the train goes past,
I love the feeling of the cold smooth glass.

Dry bread and chocolate spread and other foods such,
And the smell of coffee, that I love so much.

The gracious beauty of a droopy willow tree,
And the cuteness of my hamsters as they look at me!

All these have been my loves.

Jessica Buie (11)
Whitburn Comprehensive School

THESE I LOVE

These I love;
The clouds at sunset catching the light from the sun.   ·
With the orangey redness like crisp autumn leaves flowing
above my head.
The song of the birds singing in the trees with their sweet mellow
voices that carry with the wind.
Glistening stars that shine in the deep blue sky at night,
Water flowing through my hands sparkling as it falls.
It feels cool and tingling.
Chocolate fudge cake with a layer of icing sugar that has been
sprinkled like snow.
The taste of it is like nothing on earth, smooth and creamy from
the first bite to the last gulp.
The rough texture of the sandpaper as you rub it in your hands.
The prickly tingle it leaves behind and the sound of it as you
rub it against the wall.
And the dust that makes you sneeze.
Candyfloss wrapped around a stick that tickles your throat
when you suck it.
The colour and the shape like a big fluffy cloud.
All of these I love.

Jessica Murray (11)
Whitburn Comprehensive School

MY GREATEST MEMORIES

These I have loved
The taste of milkshake on a hot day
All the different flavours and colours
When it trickles down my throat it's like a stream of water flowing
The sight of fireworks up in the sky on a dark night
Sparkles and crackles cheers and laughter
Lots of colours that light up the sky
And the smell of the bright burning fire that warms you from the cool
cold breeze
The flames reds oranges and yellows glowing against the dark sky
My sad times when my old dog died and when I was ill lying
in my soft bed
Happy times crunching up the wrapping paper from
birthdays and Christmas
To hear the jingling sound of music and people laughing in a
crowded room
The feel of my dog's warm soft fur against my skin like a furry blanket.

Michelle Allen (11)
Whitburn Comprehensive School

MY LOVES FOREVER

I love the taste of treacle pudding and custard and the hot taste
of Chinese food on a Friday night,
The goal David Beckham scored from the halfway line,
The delight of me getting my photo taken with the FA Carling
Premier League Trophy.
All these are what I love and what I will love forever.

Sam Harrison (11)
Whitburn Comprehensive School

MY FAVOURITE THINGS

These I have loved
The taste of ice-cream just when it's melting.
It runs down my throat,
Like water running down a waterfall,
Soft, smooth, creamy and pink
Pink like a strawberry.
It goes to my head when I eat it fast,
Cold, very cold, with little icicles melting in my mouth.

The smell of freshly squeezed orange juice,
With little orange bits.
It makes my mouth water.
The little cry of that little puppy,
So small and cute,
They first bark
There first steps is all so beautiful.

Hear the children laughing and the splashing of water, cold water,
Feel the sand between your toes.
See the sun rise early in the morning,
It is so lovely and red like red rose.

Feel the lovely cool sheets on your bed
When you climb in
Soft, silky and warm after a while.

Karen Fairlie (11)
Whitburn Comprehensive School

MY FAVOURITE THINGS

These I have loved:
The taste of mother's freshly baked bread,
With its welcoming crust so crunchy and chewy and crumbling
in my mouth,
And the smell of crispy bacon on a cold winter's morning.
The shining clean white patterned plates.
The touch of the newly pressed sheets and fresh quilt all big and ruffled.
And also to see the sea, the sea and the purple orange sky
on a hot summer's evening, to see the sun setting.
To hear the sound of crisp brown leaves crunch under my feet.
Happy times going on holiday and going in the cool sea
and standing on the golden sand.
My Nanna Ray died, everyone was crying.

Suzanne Madden (11)
Whitburn Comprehensive School

MY FAVOURITES

I love the smell of the greasy fish and chips shop,
I also like the smell of black bubbly petrol.
My favourite taste is the crisp Yorkshire pud my Gran makes for me,
and the sight of fireworks makes me feel really happy.
I love the sound of a bonfire crackling in the night,
and I love the sound of people telling me I'm right.
Red, yellow, orange, and brown the autumn leaves come
tumbling down, but winter comes with ice and snow where the autumn
leaves were long ago. Autumn and winter are my favourite seasons.

Adam Sloan (11)
Whitburn Comprehensive School

THINGS I HAVE LOVED

Water, sand, the waves swooping in and out while the
seagulls fly in the blue sky.
Fur of animals, smooth, like silk, brown, black, white
ginger all different shapes and sizes.
Crash, bang thunder and lightning, rain. Lights in the sky black,
drippy, grey clouds heavy rain hitting on the window.
Round, hot, tasty, the smell of the pizza warm as it goes
down your throat.
Dark, gloomy, the crying of people's voices out loud for my Grandad.
Bright, loud, playing all day with my cat.

Sophie Ralston (11)
Whitburn Comprehensive School

MY FAVOURITE THINGS

These I have loved:
Slime, all colours, every size, every shape.
Cold metal, black, standing silently in the night's breeze.
Colourful flowers, freshly watered, swaying in the spring breeze.
The whistling wind, whirling through the trees.
Chocolate, the feeling of it melting on your tongue,
your ears crackling.
Freshly cut grass, a refreshing smell, the sound of the lawn mower
hovering over the grass.

Laura Veti (11)
Whitburn Comprehensive School

THE SENSATIONS OF MY LIFE

These I have loved:

Crackling sensation of pizza crust,
just crackles as you chew,
The juicy tomato base just makes your mouth water,
The soft, sensitive ice-cream bites, just makes you want some more,
And the twirly whirly look of the mixing mixtures.
The round floppy-shaped spaghetti,
Just wraps around your teeth.
My favourite time was out in a boat,
Just having a float,
When I caught my biggest cod.

Stephen Summerson (11)
Whitburn Comprehensive School

MY FAVOURITE THINGS

I like to feel the soft wool of a towel on my face,
I like to feel the warmth on my back from my thick quilt,
I like to hear the jingling noise of round coins in people's pockets,
I like to hear the thudding sound from an old clock,
I like to smell the heat from a burning candle,
I like to smell the sweetness of wet paint,
I like the creaminess of chocolate sliding down my throat,
I enjoy fresh bread as the crunchy crusts break,
I love smelling the sharp dusty floorboards of an open stage,
These are all my favourite things.

Paul Joyce (11)
Whitburn Comprehensive School

THE THINGS I LOVE

I like these things;
The taste of freshly baked cakes and rich melting chocolate biscuits,
The look of happy smiling faces at Christmas, sitting around the tree
receiving the Christmas gifts.
The look of first sights of spring, to hear the sound of leaves
crunching under my feet and the sounds of drums beat.
To smell the lovely red rose swaying in the breeze, and I like the
smell of fresh pot-pourri.
And to feel a fluffy towel and to feel my hair when it's
just been washed.

Melissa Saunders (11)
Whitburn Comprehensive School

THE THINGS THAT I LOVE

I like to see brown shiny chestnut horses galloping around the field.
Their glossy coats gleam in the sun as the birds cheep in the distance.
Crunchy leaves, brown red and gold falling from the trees
on to the stone cold ground.
The sight of a beautiful sunset setting over a deep blue sea.
Ice-cream, cold, smooth and creamy as it trickles down your
throat and melts and white fluffy clouds drift off in the sky.
The moon so bright and round, high above in the midnight sky.

Kyrie Geach (11)
Whitburn Comprehensive School

THINGS I LOVE

Football and canoeing I love best.
The smell of the bakers goes down my chest
and a new car refreshes me and my mar.
The shooting fireworks go up in the night
goes up, up out of sight.
The bonfire burning through the night,
the taste of chocolate mousse and apple juice.
I love the cheering of Sunderland crowd
makes me feel very proud.
The winter snow I love so when people
have snowball fights and the autumn leaves
with a fresh breeze.

David Wilkinson (11)
Whitburn Comprehensive School

THINGS I LOVE

I have loved French crusty bread and sweet crusty apple pie.
The smell of a Sunday dinner just been made.
I like eating fresh juicy pears.
I like the sound of the waves.
I like the smell of my roses in my garden.
I love to hear the birds sing in the garden
and like to see them eat bread.

Michelle Mitchell (11)
Whitburn Comprehensive School

THE BEACH

Sun, sea, sand and fun all four are rolled into one.
Ice-cream cones and hot dogs too lots of wonderful things to do.
We play in the sand we play in the sea oh what a fantastic place to be.
All day long we play and shout throwing the coloured beach ball about.

At half-past five the sun begins to hide, we collect our things
and out goes the tide.
Goodbye to the sand, goodbye to the sea, off we go home for tea.

Rebecca McDonald (11)
Whitburn Comprehensive School

THINGS I LOVE

I love the touch of soft fur going through your fingers,
The smell of bread around the baker's that lingers.
The taste of freshly baked scones and melted butter,
I like to see birds in the sky flutter.

The sight of little puppy dogs playing in the sea,
Then they come over and shake the water on me,
The taste of fresh apples just been picked off a tree.

Helen Proud (11)
Whitburn Comprehensive School

MY LOVES

These I have loved:
I love to touch damp dog's fur,
On a warm day in spring,
Soft leather with a strong leathery smell is a thing I like to touch,
I like to watch lightning flash across the sky,
To imagine being closer than I am,
A beautiful sunset with a clear golden sky,
Candles flicker in a slight warm breeze,
Like an Olympic torch burning in the wind,
The smell of bacon frying,
With a sizzling noise to go,
The fresh damp smell of new cut grass,
Floating around in a cool garden,
To hear a clap of thunder echoing round and round,
Followed by the continuous patter of raindrops,
The warm comforting sound of a fire crackling,
Waterfalls crashing down,
Like a mountain of white water,
Crystal clear,
The rough crispy feeling of sandpaper against my skin,
Smooth sand trickling through my fingers,
Thick plaited rope,
Burning and rough,
The strong leathery feeling of green leaves,
Smooth and cool,
A warm feeling of happiness spreads for good marks in a test,
It makes me glow with pride,
A last stroke of black fur,
As I say goodbye to a dearly loved pet.

Nicole Woodward (11)
Whitburn Comprehensive School